MOTHER EARTH, FATHER SKY

MOTHER EARTH, FATHER SKY

Pueblo Indians of the
American Southwest

DAVID LAVENDER

Holiday House / New York

To my wife

Library of Congress Cataloging-in-Publication Data
Lavender, David.
Mother earth, Father sky : Pueblo Indians of the American
Southwest / by David Lavender. — 1st ed.
p.   cm.
Includes bibliographical references and index.
Summary: Discusses the culture, history, and society of the Pueblos.
ISBN 0-8234-1365-9 (hardcover : alk. paper)
1. Pueblo Indians—History—Juvenile literature.   2. Pueblo
Indians—Social life and customs—Juvenile literature.   3. Pueblo
Indians—Antiquities— Juvenile literature. 4. Southwest, New—
Antiquities—Juvenile literature. [1. Pueblo Indians.   2. Indians
of North America—Southwest, New.]   I. Title.
E99.P9L38   1998   97-38119   CIP   AC
978′.01—DC21
Map by David Lindroth

Acknowledgments

Among the skilled professionals who helped bring this book to fruition were photographers Marc Gaede, George H. H. Huey, and Stephen Trimble. Among the many archivists who were involved were Arthur Olivas, Museum of New Mexico, Santa Fe; John Cahoon, Seaver Center, Natural History Museum of Los Angeles; Mona Wilson, Donna Butler, and artist Tom Gatlin of the Center of Archaeological Investigations at the University of Southern Illinois; Arthur J. Cooke, American Museum of Natural History; Mimi Dornack, National Geographic Society.

The staffs of the National Parks and Monuments were always helpful: Linda Meyers, Division of Publications, Harpers Ferry, West Virginia; Kim McLean, Chaco Culture National Historical Park; Jim Loleit, Pecos National Historical Park; Linda Morton, Mesa Verde National Park; the Western Archaeological Center; T. J. Priehs, Executive Director of Southwest Parks and Monuments Association, Tucson. Particularly helpful were displays of artifacts and other memorabilia in the visitors centers of the various parks and museums.

Many individuals helped smooth the path: Fran Hunnold, chairwoman of the board of directors, Smoki Museum, Prescott, Arizona; Dr. John Kessell, University of New Mexico, Albuquerque; Dr. Peter Steere, Special Collections, University of Arizona, Tucson; Shirley Harding, Hubbell Trading Post, Ganado, Arizona.

Assistance also came from talks with different Indians and whites who know the Indians well. Among them were Joe S. Sando, author and Director of Archives at the Pueblo Indian Cultural Center, Albuquerque; the mother-daughter team, Marie Romero and Maxine Toya of Jemez Pueblo; Ann Beckett and Tom Kennedy of the new museum at Zuni pueblo; Nancy Dahl; and several other persons we talked to here and there without learning their names. We were fortunate enough to have had fruitful meetings with the Hopi artists Victor Coochwytewa, Second Mesa, and Charles Loloma, Third Mesa, while they were still alive.

What held all this together and made it work was my wife.

Invocation

Oh, our mother, the earth; oh, our father, the sky,
Your children are we, and with tired backs
We bring you the gifts that you love.
Then weave for us a garment of brightness;
May the warp be of the white light of the morning,
May the weft be of the red light of evening,
May the fringes be the falling rain,
May the border be the standing rainbow.
Thus weave for us a garment of brightness
That we may walk fittingly where the birds sing,
That we may walk fittingly where the grass is green,
Oh, our mother the earth; oh, our father the sky.

—Tewa Indian chant as recorded at
the Museum of New Mexico,
Palace of the Governors, Santa Fe

Contents

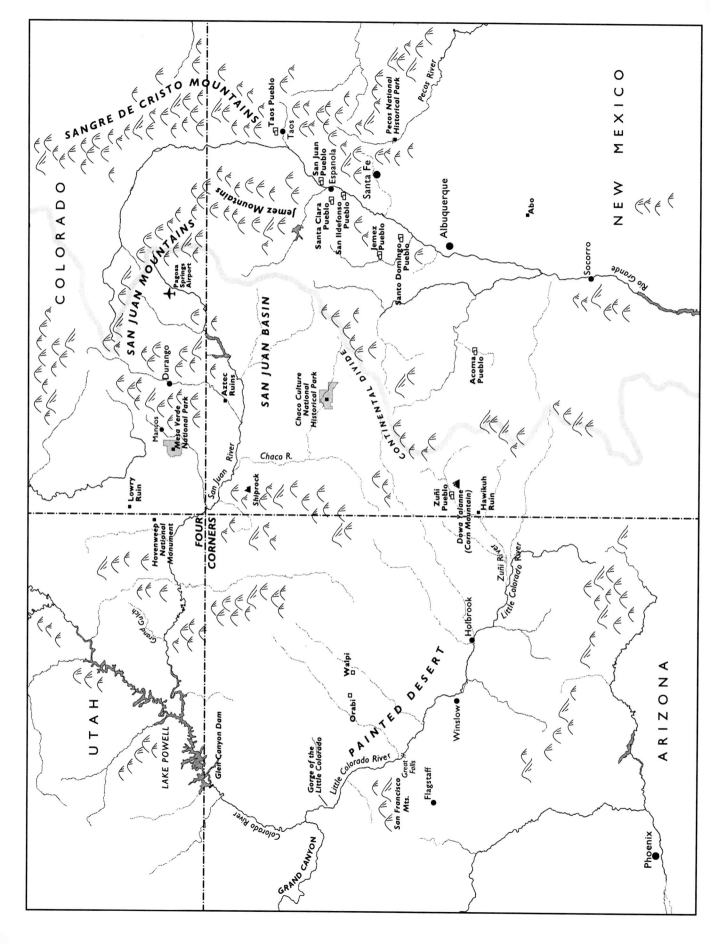

MOTHER EARTH, FATHER SKY

1

A Rough and Tumbled Land

The homelands of the Anasazi, who were the ancestors of today's Pueblo Indians, were sunbaked and windswept, gashed by canyons and freckled with cliff-girt mesas. The Anasazi themselves were equally diverse. They entered different parts of their new territory in small groups almost a thousand years ago. Several of the groups spoke different languages, as modern Pueblos still do. Yet the Anasazi's vast new territory shaped their lifestyles until they became, in many respects, very much like each other. Today's Pueblos remain strikingly similar in their customs and beliefs.

A fine way to get an overview of this dominant land is to circle it in a small plane, using different river systems as a guide. A convenient starting and ending place is the Pagosa Springs airport, nestled close to the headwaters of the San Juan River in southwestern Colorado.

Gathering tributaries as it sparkles along, the San Juan flows southwest out of thick evergreen forests into an awesome expanse of almost flat, gray-tan, nearly treeless land. This is the San Juan Basin, roughly 25,000 square miles in extent. The

The San Juan River begins near Pagosa Springs in southwestern Colorado and flows through parts of New Mexico and Utah on its way to meet the Colorado River. *Photographer, Marc Gaede.*

river, now loaded with silt, bends west beneath the plane's wings. Ahead, a great spire of volcanic stone rises out of the desert floor. Early white explorers named it Shiprock. The prehistoric Indians, who had never seen a ship, named it Rock with Wings.

A few miles northwest of the spire is another unique spot: Four Corners. Down below the plane, the states of New Mexico, Colorado, Utah, and Arizona come together at a single point, the Four Corners. Such a meeting between four states occurs nowhere else on earth.

The Indians saw nothing unique about the geography, however. To them the region was indivisible—a single vast stretch of wide-open land. Many hundreds of years ago the lands lying both south and north of the river provided living space for unknown numbers of prehistoric inhabitants.

The San Juan slides past Four Corners into Utah. Bordering cliffs begin to pinch closer and closer, until the river becomes imprisoned in the bottom of a twisting gorge. Side canyons plunge down from the high country to the north. Erosion has clawed and scraped at the tilted, stony land until it seems not even a rock wren could live there. But the Anasazi managed. They built rough homes under overhanging rocks and in the sheltered coves of spectacular Grand Gulch. The ruins of these homes are scattered throughout the gulch's twisting channel.

Not far below the mouth of Grand Gulch lies a concrete plug named Glen Canyon Dam. Behind the dam sprawls an enormous reservoir. The junction of the wild San Juan with the once majestic Colorado River lies drowned under the water of that huge storage tank. How strange! So much water is gathered where a lack of water was once the great fear of the Stone Age Indians who lived in the area.

A few miles below Glen Canyon Dam, the Colorado River begins its plunge into the world-famous Grand Canyon. The many-colored walls rise higher and higher. About seventy-five miles below the dam, the scale grows so huge that it is hard to see the string of whitish splotches where saltwater leaks out of the rock into the canyon bottom. Nevertheless, the prehistoric Indians found the place many years ago. They valued salt highly. It flavored their food and could be traded to Indians who had no salt in their lands.

In his autobiography, *Sun Chief,* Hopi Indian Don Talayesva tells of making the journey to the salt deposits nearly a hundred years ago. He was hardly more than a boy and tagged along with his father and the chief of their clan.

First the three men accumulated many feathered prayer sticks called *pahos*. They deposited these, along with offerings of yellow cornmeal, at sacred spots along the way. Many of these shrines were dedicated to Salt Mother. Salt Mother was one of the spirits who helped guard the resources provided by Mother Earth.

The three adventurers rode donkeys a hundred miles from their hometown on one of the Hopi mesas to the brink of the

In his autobiography, *Sun Chief,* Hopi Indian Don Talayesva tells of an exciting trip through the gorge of the Little Colorado to salt deposits highly valued by the Indians in the Grand Canyon.

Photographer, Marc Gaede.

Little Colorado's awesome canyon. After tying the donkeys to a clump of stout brush, they scrambled down a breathtaking trail left by previous salt gatherers. A short walk along the canyon bottom brought them to a thick growth of vegetation surrounding a large earthen dome crusted over with a hard mineral called travertine.

The three men took off their shoes and walked to the top of the sacred, fifteen-foot-high dome. There they found a hole about two feet in diameter. Peering into the opening, they saw yellow water that bubbled occasionally. They also discovered that unknown visitors had tried to measure the depth of the spring by probing it with long sticks they had left behind. The three Hopis were outraged. This was the *sipapu*, the holiest place the Hopis knew. The yellow water served as a screen to keep uninitiated people from seeing what lay below.

According to Hopi religion, the *sipapu* was the opening through which the Anasazi had climbed to reach the present or fourth world. They had made the climb because strife in the third world had destroyed the harmonies between people and the world they lived in. On reaching the fourth world, the different clans had scattered far and wide, searching for the center of the new world. There the old harmonies would be restored, if the Hopis followed the true path. During the long search, the great migrations of Hopi mythology, they had at last reached the isolated mesa where the Hopis still live.

Other Pueblo groups believe the *sipapu* is located in a different place. Wherever this holy place may be, it is near a stream or lake, for water is the heart of the Pueblos' livelihood. After giving due homage to the *sipapu*, Talayesva and his two companions continued down the Little Colorado to the Grand Canyon of the main Colorado. They followed the main river's left bank—left as they faced downstream—for a mile or so. The last stretch was along a ledge thirty feet or more above the salt deposits.

Water oozing underground along a horizontal layer of sandstone had picked up soluble salt somewhere along the way. When the buried layer of sandstone broke into the open, the water it carried formed a row of springs. The springs precipitated salt in patches along the perpendicular face of the cliff and in lumps on the rough ground.

The harvesters on the ledge tied a rope to a projecting rock. They slid down this rope to the canyon floor. Each man filled a bag with about sixty pounds of salt. One of the Hopis then squirmed back up the rope and used it to lift the bags to the ledge one by one. The other two men followed. Then back to the burros they went, and home again.

Imagine that the plane continues following the long course of the Little Colorado River toward the south and southeast. As usual, the riverbed along here is dry. Only occasionally do deluges of rain send flash floods of muddy water bellowing over Grand Falls, 125 feet high. Left and right are the many-colored knobs and vales of the Painted Desert. Off to the west the peaks of the San Francisco Mountains soar almost thirteen thousand feet high.

After flying over the modern towns of Winslow and Holbrook, Arizona, the plane reaches the junction of the Little Colorado and the Zuni Rivers. The valley of the Zuni, brightened with occasional springs of water, provided ancient traders with a gateway into and out of Anasazi country. The valley also

The Little Colorado River flows northward through Arizona until it enters the Grand Canyon.
Photographer, Marc Gaede.

nurtured the big pueblo of Zuni. The area was unusually productive. More than a century ago it provided the men and horses of the United States cavalry with thousands of *tons* of corn during their long wars with the Navajo Indians.

Not far from the town of Zuni is the sacred and extraordinarily beautiful mesa called Dowa Yalanne—Corn Mountain. The difficult trails that led to its top were relatively easy to defend, so several ancient villages had once been located there.

Now the plane increases its elevation to fly southeast across the Continental Divide. Water originating on the west side of the divide flows, if it doesn't sink into the ground first, to the

The imposing mesa Dowa Yalanne (Corn Mountain) stands in the southwest corner of Zuni country. *Western Archaeological Center, National Park Service.*

Gulf of California. Water from the east side flows into the Gulf of Mexico. The first river on the east side of the divide is the Rio Grande. It lies a few miles below the town of Socorro, New Mexico.

The Rio Grande Valley is very wide and barren here. A lot of disjointed, wrinkled mountains parallel it, especially on the east side. In prehistoric times several Indian towns occupied choice pockets in these remote uplifts. The people in these towns earned part of their living by risking trips onto the Great Plains. They hunted buffalo, which is hard to do on foot; there were no horses in North or South America during those days. When they succeeded, they came proudly home carrying plenty of dried meat and hides on their backs.

As the plane goes north, the valley gradually narrows. On both sides, the mountains grow taller and are divided into fewer segments. The Sangre de Cristo range dominates the

The broad valleys of the Rio Grande and its tributaries mark the eastern boundary of Pueblo Indian territory. *Courtesy, Marc Gaede.*

eastern horizon, the Jemez the western. Small streams splash and gurgle down the steep slopes. Because of those creeks and the river they fed, the Rio Grande region became, for a time, the most populous part of Anasazi territory.

The northernmost Indian pueblo in the Rio Grande area then, and now, is Taos. Its two "great houses" are located close to the base of the Sangre de Cristo mountains and some distance east of the Rio Grande. Probably it is the best known of the surviving pueblos. During the early 1800s, American trappers made it the starting point of their hunting trips. Today it is visited by thousands of tourists from all parts of the world.

Taos is the northernmost Indian pueblo. It is the only one that still has several stories. It stands near the foot of the Sangre de Cristo Mountains, which supply its fields with water. *Photographer, John K. Hillers, 1880. Museum of New Mexico, negative 16096.*

In effect the overview of Anasazi country is finished. One would fly back over the Continental Divide to reach the starting place at Pagosa Springs, beside the headwaters of the San Juan River. Inside the oval over which the plane traveled are thousands of ancient Indian ruins, many tiny, a few huge. Probably their full story can never be told. But one way to start is to glance at the Colorado cowboy who did so much to direct the nation's attention to the marvels the desert held—and still holds.

2

Rich with Ruins

One cold, snow-flecked day in early December 1888, Richard Wetherill and his brother-in-law, Charles Mason, rode their horses up a rocky, rough trail onto the high top of Mesa Verde in southwestern Colorado. They were looking for cattle that might have strayed from their winter range on the Wetherill Ranch. The ranch was located near the foot of the mesa, close to the Mancos River.

Instead of cattle, the two men found a marvel that drove every other thought right out of their minds.

They had ridden across a flat of light green sagebrush and into a dense stand of dark green juniper and piñon trees. As they emerged into the open again, the horses suddenly halted. Almost under their noses was the brink of a deep, narrow gorge. The men's mouths dropped open.

"Look at that!"

They should have been better prepared. Richard's brother Ben had ridden along the bottom of the gorge a few evenings before. Twilight had been thickening. He was cold and hungry,

Richard Wetherill, the first white man to enter any of the Mesa Verde cliff dwellings.
Courtesy, National Park Service.

and his horse was tugging at the reins, eager to get home. Ben had caught a glimpse of what might have been a ruin tucked into a cave high above him. He'd mentioned it after reaching the ranch, but that was all. So the two riders were as astonished as if they had been the first to have seen the marvel.

A horizontal band of whitish rimrock capped the opposite wall of the canyon. Below the rimrock a boulder-littered slope dropped steeply to the canyon bottom. In the rimrock just above the slope was a shallow cave perhaps 300 feet long. Jammed tight into the cave were clusters of partially collapsed rock houses, big round pits from which wooden ladders protruded, and roofless towers. An ancient Indian ruin, surely— but unlike any ruin the two cowboys had seen before.

There were several ruins near the ranch in the flat valley of the Mancos River. Archaeologists called them rubble mounds.

They occurred when ancient stone houses collapsed. Centuries of windblown sand and the mud of occasional floods piled up on them. Grass, shrubs, and now and then a tree took root, until the hillocks looked like ordinary mounds. Early miners and members of government exploring parties had learned different, however. An unknown people had once lived in those buried houses. Rubble mounds appear at several spots in the San Juan Basin.

Searching for souvenirs in the ruins in the Mancos area became a Sunday pastime for local settlers. They often unearthed a few stone tools, an awl made of bone, fragments of baskets, and the remnants of hard-used sandals. Once in a while the discovery of an unbroken gray clay pot decorated with geometric black designs raised a shout of joy. Such trophies made beautiful mantel ornaments, or they could be sold to tourists for a good price.

Collectors of Indian curios occasionally rented rooms at the Wetherill Ranch and hired one of the five brothers, generally Richard, to guide them to ruins they could dig in. As word of Charles Mason and Richard's discovery on the mesa spread, the number of visitors picked up. Shrewdly, Richard named the find Cliff Palace, suggesting great riches. The course of his life changed. He and other members of the family searched for and found other cliff dwellings, as he called them, tucked into other Mesa Verde canyons. They unearthed treasures of pots and mugs, beautifully woven baskets, colorful stone jewelry, and quantities of stone knives, scrapers, axes, and arrowheads. They found cloth woven of turkey feathers; they exulted over strings of turquoise beads.

Casual tourists were no longer able to absorb all the curios, so Richard sold the family's collections to museums in Denver.

An early picture of Cliff Palace, Mesa Verde, taken around 1910, looking much as it did when Wetherill and Charles Mason first saw it. *Colorado Historical Society, negative F3899.*

The Wetherill family dug into many ruins, searching for artifacts they could sell. The most common findings were utility pots, which were used for several household purposes such as storing water and cornmeal. Pots with round bottoms were kept upright by rings woven of plant fiber. *Colorado Historical Society, negative 12.*

The so-called Mesa Verde black-on-white pots were more artistic and more valuable to collectors. They were widely traded by the Anasazi, the common name for all prehistoric Pueblo Indians. *Photographer, George H. H. Huey.*

He created a fine model of Cliff Palace and displayed it at the Chicago World's Fair of 1893. Interest grew.

Newspapers speculated about "lost worlds." Reporters asked Richard endless questions. Which dwellings were the oldest, the mound houses or the cliff houses? Were the builders members of the same tribe? When had Cliff Palace been built? Richard had no answers, and trained archaeologists could offer very little help. Some people began guessing that Cliff Palace might be as old as the pyramids and mummies of Egypt—for Mesa Verde's caves contained mummies, too. One year a mummy was actually featured on a parade float that opened the county's annual agricultural fair.

Many local residents followed the Wetherills' tracks onto Mesa Verde. Eager for profits, they spread out and began digging furiously. They paid no attention to what they were destroying. To get inside a cliff dwelling, they broke through walls of elegant masonry and ripped off roof timbers, sometimes using the ancient wood for campfires.

At first Richard was as careless as the rest. But when newspapers called him a looter and vandal, he improved his work. When the wealthy Hyde brothers whom he had met at the Chicago World's Fair offered to finance an expedition into Grand Gulch, one of the wild canyons of southeastern Utah, he jumped at the chance.

Richard traveled to Grand Gulch with a long caravan. The workers, some of them Ute Indians from the Mancos area, were mounted on horses. Behind them came a string of sometimes ornery mules packed with tools and food. Richard rode in the lead. Other supervisors brought up the rear. The train entered Grand Gulch through one of the rare side canyons that carve rough pathways into the amazing red depths. The only water, except after hard rains, was in the pools fed by little springs and seeps.

Some adventurers say Grand Gulch is the most crooked gorge in the United States. Many places are so narrow that Richard's pack train could scarcely have squeezed through. Then, in scattered places, the walls pull back, making room for quiet terraces. Massive overhangs and shallow caves are abundant.

As the cold air of December 1893 began settling into the gorge, Richard stopped the caravan near a small empty stone structure under an overhang. Because of the growing cold, its excavation would be the last dig of the season. He was disappointed, therefore, when the workers found nothing unusual.

That may be why he ordered his men to keep on digging after they had reached the bottom of that stone house.

This was a lucky decision. Three feet below the floor of the cliff dwelling, the workers found twenty-eight shallow burial pits. A doubled-up skeleton, its knees pulled against its chest, filled each pit.

Obviously, the dead people had been buried before the cliff dwelling had been built. But how long before? For that matter, how old was the cliff dwelling? It seemed there was no way of telling.

But there were clues. The different groups had used different utensils. The pit people had hunted with a kind of spear called an atlatl. The cliff dwellers had used bows and arrows. The main household ware of the older group consisted of tightly woven, strikingly colored baskets. The cliff dwellers had used pottery of many shapes and sizes, but few baskets.

After noticing how different the relics were, Richard decided he had discovered a new race of prehistoric men. He called them Basketmakers.

The Hyde brothers were not impressed. They wanted richer finds. So Richard pricked up his ears when he heard talk of immense ruins several dozen miles to the south, in a bleak place called Chaco Wash or, more often, Chaco Canyon. He decided to scout the place. He loaded two wagons with supplies and attached water barrels to their sides. He told his wife-to-be and her parents to pack their traveling clothes. Then, in the fall of 1895, off they creaked.

They reached Chaco Canyon after six dry, hot, windy days of slow travel. The canyon's bottom was a mile wide. Its bordering cliffs were 200 to 300 feet high. The northern cliffs were the steepest. After heavy rains, floods would roar through a

The first shelters used by the Anasazi were alcoves in the sides of cliffs. Richard Wetherill found the first on record in Grand Gulch, a Utah tributary of the San Juan River. Because the inhabitants had no pottery, he called them Basketmakers.
Photo of a diorama in the Mesa Verde Museum. Courtesy, National Park Service.

narrow arroyo in the canyon's wide bottom. The water would drain northwest and then north to empty into the San Juan River near the towering spire called Shiprock. Since the average rainfall in the Chaco area was six to eight inches a year, there weren't many floods.

As the wagons toiled up the wash, they passed a dozen huge ruins. Some of the stone buildings had been four, even five, stories high. Most stood close to the north cliff, but, unlike the ruins at Mesa Verde, they were completely out in the open. Across the canyon and close to the south walls were many modest rubble mounds like those in the Mancos Valley. Richard was astounded. If all the ruins had been inhabited at the same time, they could have housed several thousand people. But could the barren valley have grown enough food for them? That question still hasn't been answered to everyone's satisfaction.

It wasn't the kind of question that interested Richard Wetherill. He was after mummies and other relics. Hastily he set up his first camp near the largest of the ruins. Earlier government explorers had already named it Pueblo Bonito—Beautiful Town. It was shaped like a huge *D*. The curved part of the *D* reached almost to the canyon's sheer north wall. The structure contained several hundred rooms. The big central plaza was separated into two parts. There was not a sliver of metal, not even a nail or a hinge, in either Pueblo Bonito or its neighbors.

Richard Wetherill led the first expedition to dig extensively in Pueblo Bonito, one of the "great houses" of Chaco Canyon. The picture shows the "kitchen" of some of his Navajo Indian workers. *American Museum of Natural History, negative 411854.*

Richard reported all this to the Hyde brothers. Swayed by his excitement, they agreed to finance one more expedition. Richard promptly hired several local Navajo Indians as workers. Legend says that during talks with them he asked what the Navajos called the people who had built the Chaco ruins. They said, "Anasazi." The word meant "Ancient Ones" or "Ancient Enemies."

Meanwhile, an increasing number of scientists were digging into the huge ruins of the Rio Grande Valley. Those ruins had been named pueblos by the Spanish conquerors of the region. The people who had built them were also called Pueblos. The word means "towns" and also, in New Mexico, the Indian people who live in towns. Today both words—*Anasazi* and *Pueblo*—are used to identify this culture.

The Hydes' first expedition excavated several rooms in Pueblo Bonito. They also unearthed a few of the rubble mounds on the south side of Chaco Wash. At the close of the digging season, they shipped enough relics to the American Museum of Natural History in New York City to have filled a railroad freight car.

However, trouble was developing. Amateur diggers were hurrying into Chaco Canyon, hoping for treasure. When Richard and the Hydes tried to order them away, furious quarrels broke out. All this happened while curios from many ruins flooded the market. Prices dropped. At the same time, angry citizens throughout the United States were protesting the robbing of archaeological sites they felt belonged to the whole nation.

Congress agreed. In 1906 it passed laws creating Mesa Verde National Park. The next year, President Theodore Roosevelt established Chaco Canyon National Monument. Since then its

In another camp at Pueblo Bonito, archaeologists sift through dirt taken from one of the rooms, hoping to find valuable turquoise beads. Wetherill is the man farthest to the right.
American Museum of Natural History, negative 411912.

name has been changed to Chaco Culture National Historical Park. From then on, the national park system and its rangers preserved the ruins in both areas for the enjoyment of everyone.

Such laws had become necessary, but they left some of the Southwest's pioneers, like Richard Wetherill, without jobs. To support his family—a wife and five children by then—Richard acquired a homestead beside Pueblo Bonito. There he ran a few cattle and sheep and traded with the Navajos. On June 22, 1910, he quarreled with one of those Indians about a horse. The Indian killed him with a single rifle shot.

3

Long Ago

One of humankind's greatest accomplishments has been learning how to raise crops and then distribute the harvests wisely and fairly. The first people to take that giant step lived in arid lands around the eastern end of the Mediterranean Sea. A similar triumph did not occur in the New World until thousands of years later. The reason for the delay was that vast sheets of ice, called glaciers, covered most of the northern part of the world.

Because a lot of water was locked up in that ice, the levels of the oceans were relatively low. A land bridge more than fifty miles wide connected what is now called Siberia to Alaska. Mammals, including people, crossed the bridge into the New World. Then, many thousands of years ago, the glaciers began to melt. The water rushed into the oceans, raising the level of the Pacific. Floods drowned the land bridge. The Stone Age men who had walked across the bridge to the New World were isolated from the Old World. As a consequence, they had to figure out things like agriculture for themselves.

Eleven or twelve thousand years ago, the Southwestern climate was wetter and cooler than it is now. Ponds and swamps surrounded by rushes and willows glistened in the broad valleys of the Rio Grande. Lush grasses rustled on plains that reached west into Arizona. Herds of immense mastodons, mammoths, long-horned bison, and even a species of horses fed on the plentiful plant life.

The early hunters used atlatls to hunt. An atlatl consisted of three parts: a short wooden dart, a shaft two or three feet long, and a wooden thrower. The pointed end of the dart was a carefully shaped and sharpened piece of flint or chert. The back end of the dart was pushed into a tight hollow in the front end of the shaft. The shaft hooked to the rear was the thrower. Near the back of this hinged thrower was a pair of small leather loops. The hunter inserted two fingers into the loops. He folded the thrower forward along the shaft. When he hurled the weapon, the thrower jerked back on its hinge to make a straight line with the shaft. The action not only lengthened the shaft but increased the power of the hunter's arm by about 60 percent. Modern tests show that an atlatl could deliver a relatively heavy dart with fair accuracy for about a hundred and fifty feet. The dart pulled loose from the shaft when it was embedded in the flesh of the target animal. A second dart could be quickly attached to the shaft and used to finish the kill.

The spear had no throwing stick. Its longer shaft was equipped with a detachable dart at one end. If hunters found a mammoth caught in a bog, they'd walk up close and stab it repeatedly, using a fresh dart for each thrust.

For a thousand or more years, meat was the primary diet of the first inhabitants of the Southwest. The people traveled in small family groups, following the grazing animals on which

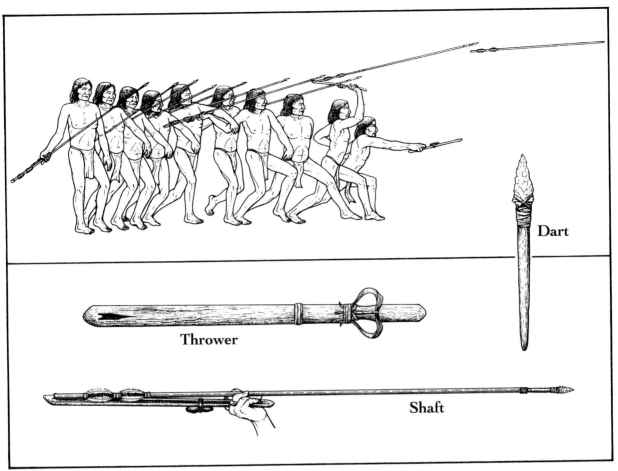

Dart

Thrower

Shaft

Before bows and arrows reached the area, the ancestors of the Anasazi hunted with spears and atlatls. An atlatl had three parts. One was a shaft two to three feet long. A dart was thrust into the front end of the shaft. Hinged to the back end was a thrower with loops for two fingers. *Artist, Tom Gatlin, Southern Illinois University, Center for Archaeological Investigation.*

Whenever the very ancient Indians found a mammoth or huge, long-horned bison mired in a swamp, they probably killed it with repeated thrusts from a spear tipped with a heavy stone point. Smaller points were used on atlatl darts.

Photographer, George H. H. Huey.

their lives depended. Then slowly, over many centuries, the climate changed. The sun blazed. The grass shriveled. Ponds dried up. The big animals drifted back to the Great Plains of the American Midwest to rejoin the vast herds from which they had originally come.

For reasons not wholly understood, most of the ancient animals in the New World, horses included, became extinct. The hunters who had followed them also vanished. During this time, however, smaller animals that didn't travel in herds—deer, antelope, and bighorn sheep—managed to adapt to the increasingly arid lands of the Southwest, as did a few small bands of humans who had not followed the other wanderers to the plains.

The many deer that have roamed in the semiarid Southwest for thousands of years have been hunted with atlatls, bows and arrows, and guns. *Photographer, Stephen Trimble.*

A culture of desert people worked its way into southern Arizona. The newcomers came from even drier lands: southeastern California, northwestern Mexico, and southern Nevada, for example. They brought with them extraordinary skills in making many kinds of baskets, sandals, rope, and other things from plants. But their great triumph was learning how to turn unlikely wild plants into food. Exactly how they figured out the process is unknown, but there are theories.

The Indians must have noticed how eagerly birds and small animals devoured ripe seeds, so it was natural for them to try eating some themselves. By looking at their own feces, they learned that the tiny pellets had passed through their digestive systems unchanged. No nutrition there.

They kept experimenting. They knew they had to crack the shells of piñon nuts to get at the tasty kernel inside. Maybe seeds, too, were covered with hard shells. Finally someone, perhaps several people in different places, tried crushing seeds between rocks. One of these rocks evolved into the metate, a flat stone whose surface had a shallow depression. The women enlarged and smoothed this trough by pecking at it with hand-held rocks. Seeds could be put into the trough and crushed by pressing down hard on a cylindrical stone, a mano, while rolling it back and forth across the seeds. The women of the family crouched on their knees in front of the metate to do this hard work.

Their reward was a coarse flour. It could be cooked to a mush by boiling water in baskets woven so tight they didn't leak; heat came from dropping hot stones into the water. Or the flour could be baked into flat cakes on other heated rocks.

The girls of the family grew up knowing the different times when the seeds of the valley and mountain plants matured.

Seeds had to be crushed to be digestible, so the women put them in a concave rock (a metate) and, pressing hard, pushed another rock (a mano) back and forth across them. The coarse meal that resulted could be boiled into a mash or baked into flat cakes. *Artist, Tom Gatlin, Southern Illinois University, Center for Archaeological Investigation.*

When the first white photographers arrived in the Southwest, Hopi women were still using rocks to grind corn into cornmeal. The butterfly hairdos showed that these millers were not yet married. *Photograph courtesy Hubbell Trading Post, negative F 10. HUT 2189.*

Guided by their mothers and aunts, they moved purposefully from plant to plant, tossing the seeds over their shoulders into a conical basket that was strapped on their backs.

Great quantities of seeds had to be stored for holding off hunger during winter and early spring. Somehow the Indians learned that unless the grain was thoroughly dried, its own inner moisture would cause it to rot or grow moldy. Again baskets came into play. The women poured the tiny grains into flat-bottomed baskets. They held the baskets over glowing embers, parching the contents bone-dry without letting the container burn.

The men meanwhile used pointed sticks to dig storage pits two or three feet deep. Digging in the sandy floor of dry caves was easy work. If no caves were handy, the diggers found a likely place out in the open near a favorite campsite. When the holes were finished, fires were built in them. The heat killed all nearby insects and hardened the surrounding earth against rodents. Often thin slabs of sandstone were added as a protec-

Seeds, a major part of the Anasazi diet, had to be parched before they could be stored. To do this, a woman held a basket containing seeds over glowing embers. She shook the basket often enough to keep it from catching fire.

Artist, Tom Gatlin, Southern Illinois University, Center for Archaeological Investigation.

tive sheathing. After the seeds had been dumped into the pit, the openings were concealed with more slabs of sandstone.

Seeds of course weren't the only plant food the Indians used. During the growing season they nibbled on fresh, tender leaves. They scraped off the tough outside covering of stalks and pounded the insides to a chewable pulp. They carefully plucked ripening flower buds off prickly cactus. They dug up wild onions and hard-to-find bulbs of sego lilies.

The men still used the atlatl for bringing down deer and bighorn sheep. But atlatls had a drawback. The hunter had to stand up out in the open to make a throw, and that often startled the quarry into leaping out of range. So they turned to smaller animals, particularly rabbits and prairie dogs. To bag them, the hunters used sticks carved like boomerangs. This stick, unlike boomerangs from Australia, did not return to the thrower. The men also fashioned snares for birds and small animals out of cords made of yucca fiber.

The most productive hunt was the rabbit drive. Two or more families would combine their long nets and stretch them out to make a big semicircle. The family members, children included, armed themselves with clubs and spread out in a line. At a signal from the "rabbit boss," who was elected to supervise the hunt, the people rushed toward the net, screeching at the top of their lungs. Many startled rabbits darted through the loose line to safety. More piled up against the net and were clubbed to death. The rabbit boss divided the rabbits among the people. The meat added protein to the Indians' largely vegetable diet. The fur was cut into strips and made into blankets or winter coats. Rabbit drives continued in parts of the Southwest until modern times.

After a thousand years or so, the camping places of these nomads could be found scattered from what is now the Mexican border north to the rugged canyonlands of southern Utah and southwestern Colorado. When archaeologists came into the region a little more than a hundred years ago, they thought they were dealing with a single race of people. But as they studied the old habitations and collected artifacts, they recognized enough differences between the regional groups to justify giving each its own name.

The southernmost were the Hohokam. East of them were the Mogollon. Elsewhere there were Hakatayas and Sinaguas. But the north is the biggest and roughest district. It was the last area to be settled by desert culture people, now called Anasazi. They came in small bands from different places and spoke different languages. But they all made extraordinary accomplishments, learning to farm and to build houses, some of them immense, out of carefully prepared stones.

4

The Magic of Maize

Corn, or maize, as the Indians called the grain, developed in Central Mexico about seven thousand years ago. It now feeds more of the world's population than any other grain except rice. That's not all. The number of cattle, pigs, and other animals that are fattened on corn is almost incalculable. The Anasazi, though, accepted it slowly when it finally appeared in their territory around 2,500 years ago.

The Anasazi had never before encountered anything like maize. Over the years they had harvested thousands and thousands of basketfuls of seed from scores of different kinds of plants. Those plants reproduced by letting go of their seeds. Some fell straight to the ground. Some were light and fluffy; they blew a long way from their birthplace before settling down. Others grew little hooks that snagged into an animal's fur or hair; those seeds were carried by the animal until something pulled them loose. Any seed that happened to land where there was good soil and a fair amount of rain was able to grow.

The development of corn brought major changes to the way the Anasazi lived. Here, a modern Hopi inspects one of his plants. *Photographer, Stephen Trimble.*

The extraordinary thing about maize is that it can't plant itself as other vegetation does. Somebody has to shuck the leaves from the cobs, which were small in those days, and scrape the kernels free. After that, the farmer has to put the kernels one by one into clusters of holes that have been punched six or so inches into the ground; the Anasazi did this with pointed planting sticks. Finally, the farmer has to hill each cluster; that is, he heaps up a little mound of earth above each group of kernels. This must be done while the ground is still moist from winter's snow, yet not so early that late frosts might nip the tender stalks. The Anasazi would sow the maize in this way in the spring, and then the band would go on its usual summer hunting and gathering trip. They hoped that when they returned they would have enough roasting ears for a few meals.

Slowly the Anasazi learned to take better care of their fields. Working in groups, they used hoes made of the shoulder blades of mountain sheep to keep wild plants from crowding in among their crops. By this time squash had also appeared from Mexico. It too needed care. Hoeing also loosened the soil so that it could store more moisture. More important was capturing the water that fell during the noisy thunderstorms of July and August. A good portion of that rainwater slid in sheets down the steeply tilted land. The Anasazi located their fields where the runoff would spread out across them. Or they placed their clusters of maize where it would be flooded by storm water jumping over the banks of the little washes that wrinkled the mesa tops. In many places the Indians built low walls of loose rocks to guide the scarce water where they wanted it to go.

Another problem was protecting the fields from hungry deer, birds, and rabbits. Although maize and squash had broadened the Anasazi's diets, they still gathered fresh greens for summer salads and seeds, along with the corn, for eating during winter. While the hunters and gatherers were away, the younger boys and girls and some of their grandparents defended the fields from birds and animals by yelling, waving their arms, and throwing rocks with deadly aim.

Each fall the maize had to be harvested. The ears were stripped from the stalks. Many were roasted. Then the kernels were separated from the cobs, parched along with the summer's gathering of wild seeds, and stored for the winter. As more food became available, the population increased. Makeshift shelters no longer satisfied the gatherings of people. They wanted more permanent dwellings.

As might be expected, their first experiments were crude. They didn't build from the ground up. Such a style would mean cutting many logs with stone axes or carrying heavy stones long distances. Besides, they knew that several varieties of animals lived in underground dens. So the early Anasazi made their first habitations by digging downward. Several able-bodied members of a group assembled near a maize field with their pointed digging sticks. There they excavated one or two circles, each twelve to fourteen feet in diameter and a foot or so deep. They lined the inside of the circle they had dug with slabs of sandstone. They used dead limbs from nearby piñon trees to create a frame shaped like a low, upside-down cone. The spaces between the tree limbs were filled with sticks and mud.

The shallow, low-roofed places were surprisingly snug. The wind passed over them. The body heat of the people inside, fortified by a small fire in the center of the shelter, kept the room warm and smoky.

The hut wasn't used very often. Each sunny day brought the people outside. The men flaked spear points for their next hunt. The women wove brightly colored baskets or ground corn. The children played. The rude shelter became a center around which these outdoor activities were held. Along with the fields of maize, it brought a sense of permanence to the people. A new word entered their many vocabularies. Its equivalent in English was *home*.

The Anasazi kept experimenting with their homes. They

extended the diameters of the pits. They kept digging with their sticks until the average depth reached about three feet, (although in very cold places, some pits were up to six feet deep). All the dirt was carried away in baskets. To gain headroom, the Anasazi for the first time built walls above the ground. These walls consisted of stout posts circling the pit. In between the posts were pickets that helped hold an upright mix of brush and mud in place.

The next step was to build a roof using large horizontal beams. A layer of smaller rafters crisscrossed the beams at right angles. The builders finished the job with a topping of dirt, grass, and a mud plaster.

Gradually the shelters deepened. The builders used digging sticks to loosen the soil. They carried away the dirt in baskets. By adding a low, wood-and-clay superstructure above each cavity, they created pit houses.

Artist, Tom Gatlin, Southern Illinois University, Center for Archaeological Investigation.

Smoke escaped from the pit house through a small, square hole in the roof. People and fresh air entered through a short tunnel at the base of the structure. A deflector stone stood on edge between the inner entrance to the tunnel and the fire pit in the center of the room. The deflector spread the tunnel's draft throughout the space. The floors of many pit houses also contained a small hole on the opposite side of the fire from the deflector. This was a *sipapu* and was symbolic of the opening through which the first people had climbed into the present world. Family rituals may have been held around the *sipapu*.

Pit houses located near cliffs are called talus houses. At first, all pit houses were entered through a short tunnel. That soon changed to entry holes in the roofs. *Photograph of a diorama in Mesa Verde Museum. Courtesy, National Park Service.*

Gradually the pit houses began to cluster into villages. Some groups were small. Others consisted of as many as fifty homes sheltering perhaps two hundred men, women, and children. That many people needed a place where they could meet, talk over their problems, and perhaps hold their religious ceremonies. To meet this need, the people built an extra-large pit house. The excavation might be thirty, forty, perhaps fifty feet in diameter. The floor and underground walls were lined with masonry. A bench people could sit on during meetings ran

Big, circular, half-buried meeting places, now called great kivas, were also used by the Anasazi for religious ceremonies. As towns increased in size, so did great kivas. This one was built at Pueblo Bonito in Chaco Canyon about A.D. 1000. It was probably covered by a massive roof. *Photographer, George H. H. Huey.*

along the circling wall. Mysterious rectangular vaults built of stone stood on either side of a raised fireplace. Window holes, built just above ground level and left empty, may have let light into the big room. Huge upright posts, some as high as twelve feet tall, held the heavy, cribbed roof. Today we call such structures great kivas.

Other new crops appeared in the villages, most notably beans. A bean or two was planted in each hill of corn. The bean vines could then climb up the cornstalks. The southern villages also acquired cotton. At first, cotton was valued for its rich black seeds, a fine food. Before long, though, looms and weaving would turn fluffs of cotton into cloth.

Pottery was developed. It became invaluable. Beans, which could not be parched, were stored in large, narrow-mouthed, fat-bellied pots. Rats couldn't possibly eat through pottery to get at the beans and seeds, so the storage containers were no longer buried but kept on the surface of the ground.

Thanks to pottery, fresh drinking water could be stored inside the pit houses. Food could be boiled more readily in a pottery bowl than in a basket. No matter how tightly the basket was woven, it could not match a pottery bowl. Pots filled with water, seeds, or anything else that would pass through the narrow mouth could be wrapped in nets and carried on a person's back. Women became skilled at putting a small, circular support on their heads. They would then fit the rounded bottom of a big jar into the small support and carry the burden on the crowns of their heads. Early Anasazi pots were mostly gray and decorated, sometimes with zigzag black patterns. That didn't satisfy people with creative instincts. Soon they were inventing different shapes of pottery and decorating them with many designs and contrasting colors.

During this same period, bows and arrows replaced atlatls for hunting. Dogs had already been domesticated. They helped hunters track down wounded animals and were useful at clearing bones and spilled foods out of the village. During the time of the pit houses, wild turkeys were also domesticated. When crops were poor, the Anasazi ate the big, stupid birds. Mostly, though, they raised them for feathers, which could be woven into robes that may have been used during special occasions. It is said that the turkeys could be driven along in flocks, as sheep were many centuries later. At night the birds were kept in smelly, ramshackle enclosures.

The people who drove the turkeys, dug the pits, and cut the wood did not live as long as we do. A lifespan of forty or so years may have been the average. But during those years, the Anasazi worried or rejoiced over many of the same things we do. Babies were welcomed with deep happiness; the death of parents and grandparents caused grief. Fathers were anxious about producing enough food for the family. Both parents tried to make sure that children learned the rituals of worship that bound the clans and villages together.

Absorbed in their personal problems, they probably felt that day followed day without much change. But change always creeps into people's lives, and so it was with the Anasazi. They kept meeting the challenges that faced them in slightly different ways. They learned to be innovative, not always following the past but experimenting a little bit, with their eyes on the future. They succeeded remarkably—at least for a while. According to one set of theories, they actually came close to creating a huge prehistoric empire in one of the harshest environments in what is now called the United States.

5

The Wooden Calendar

After a long time and in widely separated regions, one Anasazi family and then another moved out of their pit houses into new homes built on the ground surface. The walls of these homes resembled the superstructures of the abandoned pit houses. They were made of posts, pickets, sticks, and brush, all held together by cords of yucca fibers and by mud containing a scattering of fairly heavy stones. Roofs consisted of large beams crisscrossed with rafters. For the most part, the houses were contiguous and arranged in neat lines. The houses in each line shared walls. That way the rooms were easier to keep warm.

Some lines were straight; others formed arcs. Whatever their shapes, the lines faced toward one or two pit houses that were still in use. The pit houses, which were kept in good repair, served as a memory of olden times. Today we call them kivas. Considerably smaller than great kivas, these were gathering places for the men of the villages' different clans. On special

Somewhat before A.D. 1000, the pueblos in Chaco Canyon began adding more stories to the ground-level buildings. The ceilings that separated lower and upper rooms were made strong by layers of large beams crisscrossed by poles and topped with a mixture of grass and adobe mud. This room is at Pueblo del Arroyo, Chaco Canyon. *Photographer, George H. H. Huey.*

occasions, women were also invited inside. Some of the buildings' functions were religious. Kivas still play important roles in today's pueblos.

Clearly the Anasazi were moving into a new style of living. Recognizing and studying such changes is an important part of the work of modern archaeologists, because learning about other people helps us learn about ourselves. But when people of our culture deal with change, they also have to deal with

In time the Anasazi moved out of their pit houses into homes built on the ground's surface. The houses joined each other and were arranged in either a straight line or an arc. This model shows an extensive cornfield behind the community. In front are one or two pit houses retained for secret clan meetings. They were called kivas. A great kiva for larger gatherings might be built nearby. *Photograph of a diorama in Mesa Verde Museum. Courtesy, National Park Service.*

time. The ancient Indians didn't bother with time. Undoubtedly, they noticed seasonal changes, such as "the season the birds fly south" or "the season the willows bud again." But they apparently didn't have any sort of calendar that sliced time into months and days.

This frustrated archaeologists. True, they could group material objects such as pottery, weapons, building styles, and tools into related periods, but they could not date those periods. This was embarrassing. By the 1920s, growing numbers of

The Anasazi's new lifestyle is indicated by more than the change in housing. Bows and arrows replaced atlatls. At about the same time, cotton and pottery were introduced. *Photographs, George H. H. Huey.*

tourists were visiting Anasazi country, where several impressive ruins had already been designated as national parks or national monuments. Most of the visitors wanted to know when the ruins had been built and when they had been abandoned. The rangers could not tell them.

Strangely, it was an astronomer, Andrew E. Douglass of the University of Arizona, who solved the problem. He dated the ruins by examining hundreds of living trees and ancient beams throughout the Southwest.

About 1904, Douglass had begun wondering what effect, if any, sunspots have on the growth of the earth's vegetation. Sunspots are dark patches that move across the fiery surface of the sun at regular intervals.

As an offshoot of his research, Douglass learned that changes in the Southwest's weather patterns bring about corresponding changes in the growth rate of evergreen trees. Above-average rainfall in any particular year brings about above-average growth. During dry years, growth slows down. These reactions are particularly noticeable among ponderosa pine and piñon trees. These two species are the ones the Anasazi used most frequently in their buildings.

Each tree's annual growth can be determined by the alternating pale and dark rings on the cross section of the trunk. Together each pair forms what is known as a tree ring. Each tree ring shows how much the tree grew during a particular year. The growth of all the evergreen trees in a given area is the same during the same years.

Douglass conjectured that wet years produced broad tree rings; drought produced narrow rings. An examination of records kept for many years by weather stations throughout the region proved he was right. He even invented a core drill that enabled him to remove plugs of wood from ancient beams he wanted to study. That way he obtained the data he needed without removing whole beams and wrecking the buildings.

By matching the inner ring patterns of newly cut trees with outer rings in old beams used in Spanish churches, he would be able, he hoped, to date the year in which the church had been built. Written records stored away in the church library proved that once again he was right. From the churches he moved to prehistoric pueblos, using his core drill to obtain the wood samples. In a long, patient survey, Douglass and his associates were able to date Anasazi relics that had been used almost two thousand years ago. Sometimes all he had to go on were burned beams, since the dry wooden roofs of the pit houses often caught fire from sparks swirling up from the fire pits inside. Fortunately, charcoal decays very slowly, and small pieces of charred wood are often easier to read than cores taken from decaying beams.

During the 1920s and 1930s, Andrew E. Douglass of the University of Arizona figured out a way to tell the exact year that trees were cut down for use in ancient buildings. Dating the pueblos themselves—a major step forward for archaeology—then became possible. *Courtesy, Dr. Peter Steere, Special Collections, University of Arizona.*

There were problems, of course. Ring patterns show when a tree was cut down, not when it was used, or reused, in an ancient pueblo. That problem could generally be solved by comparing the ring patterns of several beams in the same site. By also studying pottery types, ornaments, bone tools, and other artifacts, a calendar for every major Anasazi ruin could be prepared. From then on, tourists almost always got their answers.

6

The Great Temples of Chaco

Mountains encircle the 25,000 square miles of the San Juan Basin in northwestern New Mexico. Otherwise, the land is, in general, tiresomely flat. Summers are fiercely hot; wind fills the spring air with dust; winters are numbingly cold. Rainfall averages a desolate eight inches a year. A common remark is, "There is sure a lot of nothin' out there."

No archaeologist would agree with that statement. The San Juan Basin embraces the ruins of hundreds of prehistoric houses built of stone. Two of those ancient dwellings were five stories tall in places and held more than five hundred rooms each. Trade in turquoise flourished. Extensive water systems captured and distributed the region's erratic rains. Roads up to thirty feet wide and as straight as an arrow's flight once scarred the sunbaked soil. Roads? How extraordinary for people who had never even imagined a wheel and owned neither horses nor donkeys to help them with their burdens.

Tree rings show that the frenzy of construction that created these marvels lasted from about A.D. 950 to about 1150, with

49

the biggest push coming a thousand years ago, during the 1000s. Then the system fell apart, and the Anasazi simply packed up and walked away from the wonders they had created.

An archaeologist, then, might remark, "Actually, there's a lot out there. We don't know much about it, but we can tell you what some of the mysteries are."

A few prehistoric people had managed to live and raise families in parts of the San Juan Basin for thousands of years—big-game hunters, seed gatherers, basket makers, and dwellers in pit houses. Then, as the population increased elsewhere and a need for new cornfields grew urgent, migrants in search of better opportunities began moving into the lonesome country. They brought with them bows and arrows, ornaments and pottery, ceremonial drums and flutes, stone axes, obsidian knives, and jars full of seed. When the travelers settled down, most of them chose not to build pit houses again but to live on top of the ground in clusters of small rooms constructed of stone. However, each of the different clans did build at least one kiva, a belowground meeting place resembling a pit house. There they could observe their ancient religious rituals.

Some archaeologists estimate that the incoming Anasazi may have built as many as four hundred villages during their stay in the basin. Most buildings were small. A few were extraordinarily big. The center of the widespread activity was a ten-mile stretch of Chaco Wash, sometimes called, grandly, Chaco Canyon. It rises in the eastern mountains and wanders northwest and north to meet the San Juan River near the flaring volcanic pillar called Shiprock.

Chaco is not a dramatic canyon. Its mile-wide bottom is flat and sandy. It is bone-dry most of the time. The actual streambed, when there is a stream, is a narrow ribbon in the canyon bottom. Today the ribbon is a gash—an arroyo about fifteen feet deep. A thousand years ago it was probably a shallow channel, shaded with willow brush and full of tough, coarse reeds. The south side of the canyon is a string of rounded hills. The north wall is a vertical cliff about 200 feet high.

Anasazi wanting to ascend or descend the cliffs behind the great houses of Chaco used stairways chipped into the rock. This is Jackson Stairway, named for the early American explorer and photographer William H. Jackson. *Museum of New Mexico, negative 81733.*

That cliff helped make Chaco world famous. From its top the land slopes upward for about half a mile to another natural barrier, this one low and ragged. The tilted space between the two obstacles is unusually barren, even for the San Juan Basin. Its surface consists of broad, flat patches of naked rock alternating with hard, sand-topped soil where only a few bushes grow.

Summer rains batter the Chaco area without apparent rhyme or reason—a crash of wetness here, another there, to the tune of ferocious lightning explosions. Then in a matter of minutes, the swollen clouds move on. During those minutes, rain falls in torrents. Unable to soak into the ground, the water races wildly into a network of shallow ravines. These carry the muddy flood to the rim of Chaco's north cliff. Over it goes—a bountiful waterfall.

Over tens of thousands of years, the plunging water carved out short branch canyons leading into the main Chaco streambed. To the inventive Anasazi who congregated in the area, the surges of water looked like blessings from the gods. It was their duty, they thought, to make the most of them.

Construction experts working with tools of stone and wood built a sturdy diversion dam near the feet of about twenty waterfalls. The largest dam, it has been calculated, was 120 feet long, 7 feet high, and 20 feet thick at its base. A stone-lined exit gate concentrated the flow into a canal about 9 feet wide and almost half that deep. That canal and the others in the vicinity could have delivered water to perhaps ten thousand little gardens . . . *if* water poured into every branch canyon every summer.

The possibility of always having ample water brought several dreams into being. It is hard to say which idea developed first. Perhaps the projects were undertaken more or less at the same time, although this would have put a big strain on the Anasazi labor force.

One activity was the creation of a widespread trade network. Its basic commodity was a semiprecious blue-green jewel called turquoise. Somehow, the Chacoans gained control of turquoise mines south of the present-day city of Santa Fe. Traders carried the raw ores to the line of small pueblos located on the south side of Chaco Wash, opposite the point where several massive structures were probably already taking shape. There, craftsmen converted the gemstone material into handsome strings of beads, pendants, earrings, and bracelets. They created art objects out of turquoise inlaid in jet or wood. They made religious figurines and effigies of the same material.

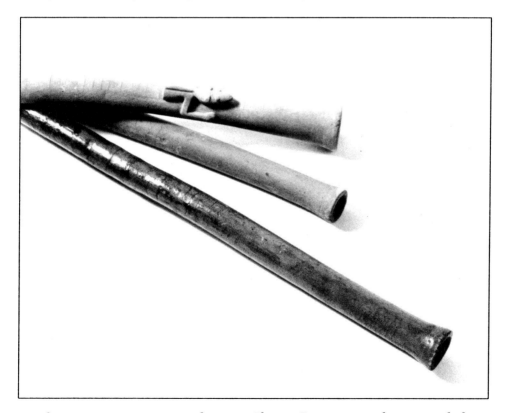

Trading parties entering or leaving Chaco Canyon may have traveled to the music of flutes like these. Note the lizard-head decoration on the top flute. *Photographer, George H. H. Huey.*

Some of the gemstones were no doubt traded throughout the basin for fine sandals, cotton blankets that weavers were beginning to turn out on their looms, and perhaps fresh evergreen boughs, which were always in demand at ceremonial functions. Most of the artwork, though, went south. Although the Anasazi traders may not have reached Mexico in person, they certainly met parties of Mexican traders carrying objects they were eager to swap: little copper bells, seashells from the Gulf of California and the Pacific, brightly colored parrot feathers, and, more than likely, salt from the Zuni area.

Meanwhile, skilled workers were pushing the walls of the great houses higher and higher. The three largest were located close to the north cliff within a space of less than a mile. The central one, now called Pueblo Bonito (Beautiful Town), contained at least 650 rooms. An unknown number of others, along with part of the pueblo's fifth story, were wiped out in 1941 when a piece of the canyon wall collapsed.

For thousands of years, sandals woven out of tough plant fibers were the Anasazi's only footwear.
Photograph, George H. H. Huey.

After Pueblo Bonito was abandoned in about A.D. 1200, the topmost stories began to crumble away. With a few exceptions, only the roofless houses and kivas of the ground floor remain to be excavated. *Photographer, David Six, National Park Service.*

D-shaped Pueblo Bonito may have looked like this while it was flourishing during the early 1100s. *Artist, Kenneth Conant. Courtesy, National Geographic Society.*

Half a mile east of Bonito was Chetro Ketl. It too reached five stories in places and contained 500 or more rooms. Pueblo del Arroyo, the smallest in this stretch, was the last one built. Perhaps it was designed to meet the Anasazi's demand for more lodging places. It was only a quarter of a mile west of Pueblo Bonito. It reached four stories in height and contained at least 285 rooms.

On top of the north mesa and two-thirds of a mile back from the canyon's brink was Pueblo Alto (High Town). Pueblo Alto seemed almost a pygmy—one story, 133 rooms. But it was the gateway to the three principal buildings in the canyon. Roads from all parts of the northern San Juan Basin converged at the mesa-top town. At certain times of the year, great numbers of travelers apparently assembled at Pueblo Alto with their goods. They were feasted and then sorted out for marching down stairways carved into the cliff to visit one of the three great buildings below—Chetro Ketl, Pueblo Bonito, or Pueblo del Arroyo.

There must have been access routes from the south as well, but the details have not been worked out. It should be noted that there were other sizable pueblos in the area, but the ones described here were the leaders. The people they drew may have gathered for trade, politics, or, most probably, religion.

For centuries, the Anasazi enlarged buildings by adding a room or two whenever they felt the need. The Chacoans, however, learned to plan in advance. The design of the walls at Pueblo Bonito and Chetro Ketl, for instance, show that the native architects planned from the beginning to create the most impressive structures in the ancient Southwest. The bases of those walls are very thick, so the workers must have known in advance that the walls were going to have to support the weight of several stories.

First, the builders erected an ordinary wall as wide as a single, good-sized chunk of rock. They used plenty of mud to cement the wall's rocks together. Then they surrounded both sides of that rough wall with a veneer of small, flat, very hard, carefully shaped stones. Gaps between layers were carefully chinked. Protruding edges were smoothed away. The results were strikingly handsome. But that wasn't enough for the Chacoans. They disguised the veneer by covering all the exposed walls with a thin plaster of mud from which all lumps had been removed. Clearly they meant to impress visitors by presenting them with rock walls as smooth as polished turquoise gems.

Both Chetro Ketl and Pueblo Bonito were shaped like the capital letter *D,* as indeed were most of the big houses in the vicinity. The curve in Bonito's *D* reached back almost to the northern cliff. Chetro Ketl's very shallow *D* faced in the opposite direction, toward the streambed in the canyon. Both structures embraced wide plazas. Each plaza contained several ordinary-sized kivas and a great kiva or two. Additional kivas occupied prominent places in the room blocks themselves.

Every room and every kiva had to have a roof. Every roof consisted of large horizontal beams crossed at right angles by smaller beams covered with grass and mud. Piñons furnished logs for many of the beams. Larger beams came from ponderosa pines. The roof supports of great kivas were generally large posts twelve feet high and two feet in diameter. One archaeologist estimated that five thousand trees were used in the construction of Chetro Ketl alone.

The trees were cut down and trimmed with stone axes. The end of each log must have looked as if it had been chewed by beavers—much too ragged for a jewel-like building. So the ends were carefully sanded smooth by hand.

The enormous amounts of wood needed in the pueblos (firewood included) were patiently hewn out of distant forests with stone axes like this one. *Photographer, George H. H. Huey.*

Suitable forests lay about forty miles away, east and west. Every beam and kiva post and all firewood had to be carried to the canyon by sweating gangs of workers. They must have believed very strongly in the worth of what they were doing.

The rows of rooms in each major pueblo were terraced (Pueblo Alto had only one floor). That way the workers could stand on the roof of one floor while building the walls of the one above it. Everything they used—rocks, beams, adobe clay, and innumerable jars of water for turning the clay into mortar—had to be carried up ladders.

Many of the outer rooms on the lower floors were closed

except for doorways leading from one into another. Some of those dark cells were filled to the roofs with corn and beans. Both the residents of the pueblo and outsiders could depend on the stores during times of hunger. Much of the town's trash—sweepings, garbage, broken household goods—were packed into other rooms. There were also great trash mounds outside the pueblo.

Only a few of the rooms were used as residences. Archaeologists reached this conclusion because of the few skeletons they found. During scores of years, the excavations at Pueblo Bonito, Chetro Ketl, Pueblo del Arroyo, and Pueblo Alto yielded a total of only 121 burials, yet their total population was supposed to be in the thousands. Perhaps the cemeteries had been destroyed by erosion or covered by silt deposited by floods.

The archaeologists checked the hundreds of rooms they had excavated for clues to burial sites. What they found instead is that a large number of rooms, particularly those larger than average, lacked the prime essential of home living: a fire pit for cooking and warmth.

Their conclusion was that the huge structures had been built to awe the ordinary people. They were places of worship. Only caretakers stayed in them permanently. Other people came only at certain times of the year to go through their age-old rituals. The rituals, they believed, would persuade the gods to keep on sending them what they needed most—good weather, especially rain. Without rain to bring their crops to life, they could not survive.

The theory helped explain the mysterious straight roads that ran from settlement to settlement throughout the San Juan Basin south of the San Juan River. Modern developments in the

Excavating large ruins required the moving of lots of dirt. Workers at one of Chetro Ketl's great kivas met the problem with a system of pulleys and a mine car that ran on tracks to an out-of-the-way dump. *Museum of New Mexico, negative 66986.*

basin, such as livestock grazing, farming, and drilling for oil and gas, have destroyed many miles of the roads. But even more miles have been revealed by low-flying airplanes loaded with high-tech cameras and other sensing devices.

No doubt traders used the roads to go from one town to another. Woodcutters took advantage of any stretch of smoothness that ran beside a forest. Food probably passed back and forth. The main traffic, though, probably consisted of large groups of pilgrims traveling to the great buildings that represented the heart of their beliefs, much as cathedrals and synagogues represent the beliefs of many today. Often the pilgrims traveled at night, guided by great fires built on the top of lookout points.

Surely a complex organization was needed to run the system. Surely certain chiefs acquired great power and used the power to hold the people together. Conceivably the Anasazi were at the point of creating a prehistoric empire in one of the bleakest regions of the Southwest.

The system could not withstand real trouble, however. The hard-used cornfields in the canyon bottom grew less and less productive. The last wood within reasonable reach was stripped. Then in A.D. 1130, a severe drought set in. Grasslands dried up; game animals vanished. People began quarreling over the last supplies of corn. Outlying villages began to defy the control of the Chaco chiefs. How could the gods let so many things go wrong so suddenly? Faith in the old rituals diminished. The people began to leave. Some probably went south to what became Acoma, and to the land of the Zuni. Others pushed east to the Rio Grande Valley with its alluring river. By A.D. 1200, as far as we can tell, no one was left in the basin south of the San Juan River.

Slowly the great temples of Chaco began to crumble.

7

The Cliff Dwellers

The middle part of the great Mesa Verde tableland is about 7,300 feet higher than sea level. Because of this altitude, the central section of the mesa receives roughly eighteen inches of precipitation during normal years, more than double the amount that splatters Chaco Canyon during a comparable period.

Additionally, the mesa's big, rectangular surface slopes toward the south. Sunshine washes across the land throughout the winter. Warmth comes early in the spring. The growing period for crops planted on the mesa stretches out to an amazing 167 days. Areas two thousand feet lower, at the foot of the mesa, have shorter growing periods.

Attracted by the climate and long growing season, small parties of Anasazi farmers struggled up the steep trails to the mesa top between A.D. 600 and 700. The new settlements on the forested mesa followed the same pattern of development the Anasazi used in Chaco, where the nearest trees were many miles away. First came pit houses. Then gradually some of the

Indians decided to build homes on the ground's surface. Those first fragile stick-and-mud huts evolved slowly into lines of adjoining stone houses. Eventually the lines of houses reached out to embrace a space we call a plaza. Most of the town's social and religious activities took place on the plazas.

High altitude and relatively heavy rainfall created special problems. To fight the winter cold, the Mesa Verde pit houses were six feet deep, twice the depth of those at Chaco. Runoff from melting snow and summer thunderstorms dug a series of deep parallel canyons into the mesa top. Because of those

The people of Mesa Verde built their many cliff dwellings with intensive labor during the 1200s. No one is quite sure why these people suddenly left. Many of them crossed the Continental Divide and settled along the Rio Grande. This picture is of Cliff Palace, which has been partially restored for modern tourists. *Photographer, Marc Gaede.*

gashes, the Mesa Verde people could not build roads like those at Chaco. Consequently, Mesa Verde's trade was never as extensive as Chaco's.

Abundant moisture fostered the growth of thick forests of juniper and pine. Using stone axes, the Mesa Verdans cleared out wide swatches for their crops. The cleared trees yielded plenty of wood for construction and fires.

Fine pottery might also be considered a Mesa Verde crop. The women controlled the entire process. First, the potter prepared moist, smooth clay. To this she added temper. The temper might have been ground-up grains of volcanic rock or even broken pieces of old pottery. The mixture kept the pot from cracking as the clay cooled after being hardened in carefully arranged fires.

The pots were formed out of coils of this tempered clay. The coils were wound upward and outward according to the image the artist had in mind. If a pot was intended for household use—cooking, storing corn, holding drinking water—the outside surfaces of the coils might be pinched together to give the vessel the corrugated look the Mesa Verdans favored. If a pot was for home decoration or trade, the maker would rub and rub and rub the inside and outside surfaces with a cherished polishing stone to produce a vessel whose walls were as smooth and thin as possible. The artist then prepared a black paint from wild plants such as beeweed. Using a brush of yucca fiber, she drew complex geometric designs on the outside surface of the pale gray pot. Modern archaeologists call these ceramic creations of Mesa Verde "black-on-white." Then came the firing, a tricky business with the pot entirely surrounded by burning fuel.

Some large pots had round bottoms. The people made them

stand up by putting the bottoms into little holes scooped in the floor of the house. A sort of cup made of stout plant fibers could also hold the round bottoms steady.

Women could carry amazingly big pots on their heads, even up ladders. But it was safer to put large pots in a bag or a net and sling them over their shoulders.

Clay vessels were hard but brittle. Breakage was common, but production was enormous. Pot-hardening fires became another drain on the wood supply.

As the population increased, too much wood disappeared. Heavy plantings of corn sucked most of the nourishment from the bare soil. Hard rains caused further damage. With no trees and little brush to slow runoff, ton after ton of topsoil washed away into the canyons.

As production shrank, worried people scattered out across the mesa, looking for new places to live. About the year A.D. 1200, the majority of them decided to move into various horizontal caves that marred the sides of the canyons. Today there seems to be no wholly satisfactory explanation for this sudden widespread movement.

One suggestion is that the Anasazi were naturally restless, especially after the recent abandonment of Chaco. Or perhaps their shamans thought they could help renew the abused earth by going back into the earth themselves.

Or they may have panicked.

Imagine what would have happened if a few small groups of Chaco Anasazi had remained behind when most had left the southern part of the San Juan Basin. The deserted ones may have tried to keep on living in their familiar towns, but things in general must have fallen apart. To support themselves, lonesome Chacoans moved north across the San Juan River to regions where many Anasazi still lived. They became brigands, launching surprise raids on small settlements, driving the inhabitants away and living on their produce until it was gone. Then they hunted for new prey.

This sort of action had been unknown among the Anasazi. Bewildered, they decided to seek safety by moving into caves that could easily be defended. The flight spread from Mesa Verde to other sections that contained caves—smallish ones in the twisted gorges of southern Utah, larger ones in Skeleton Mesa west of the present-day Navajo town of Kayenta in northeastern Arizona. If there weren't caves, the refugees moved out on the ends of high, precarious, rocky ridges. Other hideouts were built on the tops of almost unscalable cliffs. The people of Hovenweep, west of Mesa Verde on the Colorado-Utah border, tried still another experiment. They clustered along the rims of small canyons, hardly noticeable from a distance, where springs of water oozed from the rock. There they built watchtowers where the people could assemble and fight if necessary.

The Hovenweep people, who lived west of Mesa Verde, built stone towers on the edges of narrow little canyons that held springs of precious water. Suddenly they too left their homes and followed the Mesa Verde migrants. *Photographer, Jesse Nusbaum. Museum of New Mexico, negative 60695.*

The hidden stone granaries were stranger yet. One, two, three, or even more miniature rooms were perched on high, dizzy ledges and then filled with corn. The granaries and the cliffs they huddled against were the same color, so the structures were all but invisible. It seems that the purpose of these hidden granaries was to provide supplies of food to fall back on in case bandits drove the builders away from their normal supplies.

Archaeologists have devoted most of their attention to Mesa Verde's numerous caves. Most were located high in the canyon walls. Some were several hundred feet long, dozens of feet high, and deep enough to hold rows of tightly crowded houses. Preparing them for habitation was an exhausting chore.

First, several pioneers cleaned out the interiors and leveled the floors by packing in dirt behind retaining walls. House builders hauled up rocks from the foot of the cliff or helped themselves to already shaped stones in abandoned villages on the mesa top. They tore the wooden beams they needed out of the same villages. They placed their kivas near the outer edge of the cave's floor. The dark inner parts of the cave were used for turkey pens, trash bins, and latrines.

Rooms were barely big enough for a grown Anasazi to stretch out to full length. Old people and small children were constantly in danger of falling out of the higher caves into the canyon bottoms. So were the people who used ladders and rows of tiny footholds for carrying food, fuel, and water across the perpendicular faces of the cliffs. Clear winter days were warm, but at night fires had to be kept burning throughout the cliff dwellings, as the cave towns came to be called.

Not many years after the cliff dwellings had been completed, the townspeople suddenly moved out of them. The abandon-

Keet Seel, in Tsegi Canyon, a few miles northwest of today's Kayenta, Arizona, was occupied for fewer than ten years before it was abandoned in about A.D. 1300. The black streaks are minerals deposited by oozing water. *Photograph courtesy, Western Archaeological Survey, National Parks, Tucson, Arizona.*

ment occurred toward the end of the 1200s. The towers of Hovenweep and every other defensive hideout in the Anasazi region were also deserted. Some of the movers went south and southwest to join the Hopi and Zuni bands and perhaps to participate in the building of a "sky city" on top of the great rock bastion of Acoma. The majority of the new migrants, however, crossed the Continental Divide at various passes and swelled the growing population of the Rio Grande Valley.

Again, reasons for the shift are hard to pin down. A drought prevailed during the last quarter of the 1200s, but tree ring studies indicate that it was no worse than other dry spells the Mesa Verdans had survived. Other studies suggest that temperatures in the Southwest dropped enough to make the ripening of corn uncertain.

The most powerful reason for the migration may have been rumors of a new religion. Stories circulated of new rituals that, if performed properly, would persuade the gods to restore harmony to the people and fertility to the earth. The Anasazi of

Other fugitives probably went to Zuni Pueblo. One attractive ceremony there involved Shalako dancers whose faces were hidden by extra-tall headdresses. The Shalakos visible beyond the watchers in this picture are standing on the ground, but they tower over the crowd. *Photographer, Ben Wittick. Museum of New Mexico, negative 39349.*

The people from the Keet Seel area may have been fleeing from drought and raiders, or they may have been drawn south by the new kachina religion that had recently captivated the Hopis. This relatively new picture is of the Hopi town of Oraibi, one of the oldest continuously settled towns in the U.S. *Seaver Center, Los Angeles Museum of Natural History.*

the north certainly needed to bring such qualities back to their lives. But they may not have heard the promises before they had reached their new homelands in the Rio Grande Valley and its tributaries in roughly A.D. 1300. No matter. Wherever and whenever the Anasazi first came into contact with the kachina faith, as it was called, it became a powerful element in helping them adjust to their new environment.

Not a single Anasazi lived in the entire San Juan Basin after A.D. 1300. Not a soul stepped through these laboriously built doorways. No one needed a ladder. The abrupt dispersal is perhaps the most intriguing mystery of the Pueblo civilization.

Photographer, George H. H. Huey.

8

From Outer Space

New outbreaks of terror did not disturb Pueblo lands for another 250 years—approximately the same number of years the United States has been a free nation. The Pueblo Indians used the time to bring their civilization to a new peak.

Magnitude was the most noticeable characteristic. Enough people moved into the Zuni area to create six compact villages, some of them with buildings five stories tall. Several ancient trails converged on the area, turning it into a flourishing trade center.

Another bustling trade complex was the dozen or so Hopi villages located on the southern fringes of Black Mesa in northwestern Arizona. Hopi success depended, in part, on what might be called hidden water. The high areas of Black Mesa lay in the north. Moisture that fell there, either as rain or snow, collected in underground channels and drained south, emerging where the ragged fringes of the mesa broke down into the desert. Windblown sand, trapped by the dwindling cliffs, buried the emerging springs. Sand, however, is more likely to protect water than to absorb it. The Hopis discovered the hidden springs and learned to raise abundant crops by planting the seeds six inches deep in sterile-looking sand.

The Hopis also discovered veins of coal just under the rocky surface of Black Mesa. Using primitive tools, they scraped away the surface and became America's first coal miners. They used chunks of the black stuff for heating their homes and for firing their orange-red pottery, prized as trade items.

By far the greatest number of people lived along the Rio Grande and its principal tributaries. There were probably more than a hundred villages in the two-hundred-mile stretch between Taos in the north and present-day Socorro in the south. Most of the multistoried room blocks were built of stone. Where adequate amounts of stone were unavailable, the Indians mixed dry grass into adobe mud, let it dry hard under the sun, and used those bricks in their buildings.

Some of the pueblos were huge—up to three thousand rooms in a few places. Such a town was probably divided into two or more blocks of rooms, sometimes called great houses by archaeologists. Each rectangular unit was built around a sunny plaza, where most daily living took place.

One or more kivas were located in each plaza. In those murky depths, men—and only men—delved into the secrets of the new kachina religion. According to that religion, every object in the world—plants, rocks, animals, clouds—was believed to contain an invisible spirit called a kachina. These spirits were not deities; they were messengers who carried word of the Pueblos' greatest needs to the deities—needs such as rain, good harvests, good health, and, above all, peace and harmony for the world.

The kachinas, the Indians believed, visited the pueblos

for half of each year, from late fall through the following spring. Because they could not be seen, they were impersonated by Pueblo worshipers using elaborate masks and colorful costumes. Communication between people and spirits emerged through complicated ceremonies and foot-stamping dances timed to chants or the beat of drums. The rituals were performed in the kivas and, at times, in the plazas. Other dances, also accompanied by chants or drumbeats, were occasionally held in the plazas during the half of the year when the kachinas were at their homes on mountaintops. These summer dances were mainly for entertainment. No masks were worn; no kachinas were impersonated.

The kachina ceremonies helped unite the different clans, and the medicine and hunting societies, within a village. But nothing united the different pueblos with each other. Part of the separateness occurred because various pueblos spoke different languages. But even towns speaking the same language paid scant attention to each other. This self-imposed isolation sometimes proved to be a fatal weakness.

At about the same time that the Anasazi of Mesa Verde and Hovenweep were drifting into the Rio Grande Valley, parties of Apache Indians from the north were beginning to occupy the High Plains country of eastern New Mexico. The newcomers lived in tall, pointed tepees made of buffalo skins stretched over circles of poles leaning inward. Although the Plains Indians had no horses yet, they were expert hunters.

Large, fierce, well-trained dogs were their beasts of burden. Each dog pulled a contraption called a travois (tra-'voi). An owner would attach one end of a pair of tepee poles to each side of his dog. The other end would drag on the ground. A platform of sticks and straps was built between the lower ends of the poles. When the Apaches traveled, they piled their tepees' skin coverings and other household items on as many travois as they needed. Sometimes, too, they strapped packs directly onto the dogs' backs.

As soon as the Plains Indians (which included Navajos, a branch of the Apaches) met the Pueblos, they began trading with them. The newcomers liked the cotton cloth woven by the men of the southern pueblos. They relished corn, which they did not grow themselves, and they wanted pottery of all kinds. In exchange they offered buffalo skins, buffalo horns for ceremonial use, and dried meat. They also swapped arrows whose points were made of specially hard, carefully sharpened rock.

Pottery was an important article of trade. Each town had its own distinctive style. Women were the potters, although men often helped with digging up the right kind of clay and sometimes lent a hand at painting designs on the pots before they were fired. *Seaver Center, Natural History Museum of Los Angeles County.*

Among the Pueblo Indians, men are the weavers. This craftsman is making a sash. *Seaver Center, Natural History Museum of Los Angeles County.*

The main trading centers were Taos in northern New Mexico and the awesome pueblo of Pecos, some twenty-five miles southeast of present-day Santa Fe. It is said that on trading days scores of people driving as many as five hundred packed dogs would visit Pecos. After bargaining was over, the traders of Taos and Pecos would keep what goods they wanted and send the rest to the distribution centers of Hopi and Zuni. They did not use dogs for this distribution. Up to fifty men would carry the loads on their own backs. Often they played haunting tunes on their flutes as they traveled.

Children gather on the round top of one of the kivas at the great trading center of Pecos. The Pueblo rose tall and strong beside the trail that linked the Rio Grande Valley and the High Plains of eastern New Mexico.

Artist, Roy Anderson. Courtesy, Pecos National Historical Park.

The trouble with the Apaches, in Pueblo eyes, was that they were undependable. If the Apaches thought they could gain more profit by fighting than by trading, they would launch surprise attacks on one pueblo or another. They did not worry that several pueblos would join forces to strike back. Each stone or adobe town had to take care of itself.

A shattering change came in 1540. Only twenty years before that, bearded people from across the ocean had conquered the Aztec empire in Mexico. The victors were Spaniards from what was then one of the most powerful nations in Europe. They

In 1540, the first Spanish invaders appeared. Led by Francisco Vásquez de Coronado, they were looking for gold and jewels. A shaman of the Zuni town of Hawikuh drew a warning line of cornmeal across the invaders' trail to stop them. The better armed, mounted Spaniards easily won the battle that followed. *Artist, Louis S. Glanzman. Courtesy, National Park Service.*

stole from Mexicans enormous riches of gold, silver, and vast lands that could be cultivated by slaves.

When rumors of the prosperous pueblos in the north reached the Spaniards, they dreamed of another Mexico to loot. A strong expedition was put together under the command of young Francisco Vásquez de Coronado. Close to three hundred cavalrymen and foot soldiers were reinforced by an unknown number of Mexican Indian allies. The expedition took with it 1,500 horses and mules for riding and packing, terrifying animals the likes of which the Pueblos had never seen before. Another thousand cattle, sheep, and goats were driven along for food. Metal glinted everywhere; light sparkled on guns that thundered and belched smoke, on steel helmets and breastplates, on swords and knives and daggers. As far as the Pueblos were concerned, the invaders were as amazing and frightening as if they had come from somewhere out of the black spaces in the night sky.

Coronado's advance guard easily crushed the Zuni town of Hawikuh. The remaining Zunis fled to the top of their sacred

Spanish cavalrymen as portrayed by native artists in central Mexico. *Redrawn by Jerry L. Livingston. From* Kiva, Cross, and Crown. *Courtesy, Dr. John L. Kessell.*

mesa Dowa Yalanne (Corn Mountain). Next, a small detachment from the main expedition overwhelmed the Hopi. Winter was the worst time. The Spaniards spent it in the central part of the Rio Grande Valley, an area now largely covered by the city of Albuquerque and its suburbs. The invaders forced the Indians to hand over a pueblo for the soldiers to live in. They demanded that the Pueblos supply them with enough food and warm clothing for their hundreds of men.

Battles erupted. The Pueblos fought furiously, killing twenty-five or so of the Spaniards' horses. In the end, though, they were defeated. The Spaniards burned the wooden roofs off the two big towns, hanged many of the residents, and burned others at the stake.

Nothing, not even torture, persuaded the Pueblos to give the invaders any information about precious metals or jewels. That was because the Pueblos possessed no such things. However, to get rid of the invaders, they told them there might be incalculable amounts of loot in the kingdoms way out on the Plains. A large part of the Spanish expedition hurried there and found nothing.

Dispirited, the treasure hunters returned to the Rio Grande Valley. There they spent a miserable winter. During their stay, Coronado was seriously injured when his horse fell on him. In the spring the bedraggled army disappeared over the horizon, heading home empty-handed.

The Pueblos, who had been hiding in the mountains, returned to their ruined villages. Great sighs of relief passed among them. Many things were in miserable shape, but at least they'd never again see the likes of those ruthless invaders out of nowhere.

Or so they told themselves.

9

The Desperate Years

During the middle months of 1598, an enormous caravan toiled slowly up the Rio Grande Valley. It was so big and varied that it traveled in segments. Way out in front, mounted on fine horses, were the principal men. A mixed lot dragged along behind them. A few rode chunky little horses or donkeys, but most walked. Some were farmers; others were soldiers. Several were accompanied by their wives and children. There were eight Franciscan friars dressed in brown robes and sandals.

Horned oxen dragged along eighty-three heavily loaded two-wheeled carts. Far to the rear, obscured by a haze of dust of their own making, were thousands of cattle, sheep, goats, and loose horses. Keeping the herds moving was the job of fierce-looking Mexican Indian riders who had been trained as vaqueros, or cowboys. Other Mexican Indians were scattered throughout the column.

Three or four of the Mexican Indians had important parts to play. One way or another, they had been associated with three short-lived, unlicensed Spanish expeditions that had prowled around New Mexico at intervals during the preceding eighteen years. The Mexicans had picked up a smattering of the different Pueblo languages, and as a result they were going to act as interpreters for this newest group of invaders.

This new group had been authorized by the King of Spain and was wholly legal. Its commander was Don Juan de Oñate (the *Don* here is a title, not a name). His father owned rich mines in northern Mexico, so the son had been able to put together this costly expedition.

Meeting the expedition costs would be easy, he thought, if he found more rich mines or if he developed profitable agricultural and grazing lands. Furthermore, he would receive the

In 1598, Juan de Oñate led the first long column of permanent Spanish settlers up the Rio Grande Valley into the heart of Pueblo country. *Artist, Roy Anderson. Courtesy, Pecos National Historical Park.*

title *adelantado,* which means, roughly, "he who goes first." It was an honor given to very few men.

Don Juan de Oñate planned great changes for the Pueblos. They would lose their independence. The new rulers would tell them on how much of their former lands they could live. Only one religion, the Catholic religion, of which the Indians as yet knew nothing, would be tolerated. In return for accepting these new laws, the Indians would receive the blessings of civilization.

Don Juan de Oñate and the friars who accompanied him explained the Spanish program to the Pueblo leaders at a series of meetings in the Rio Grande Valley. The first of the gatherings was held at a pueblo whose name the invaders changed, without permission, to Santo Domingo. The meeting place was one of Santo Domingo's great kivas. It is said that seven important Indians representing thirty-four villages attended—in a structure soon to be outlawed.

The representatives listened carefully as the Mexican Indians accompanying the Spaniards interpreted what the white men had to say. To show that they understood, each Pueblo leader knelt and kissed the hands of Oñate and the Franciscans. No Pueblo left a record of the meeting, so we can't judge the accuracy of the Mexican Indians' interpretations. More importantly, we don't know what the Pueblos were thinking when they bowed to the invaders.

The next meeting took place, in August 1598, near the present town of Española, where the Chama River runs into the Rio Grande. By then Spanish scouts riding strong horses had visited nearly every town in New Mexico. They had decided that the river junction would be a good location for the capital city of the new Spanish province.

The invaders needed a place to live while erecting both the capital building and New Mexico's first Christian church. As a dwelling place for the workers, Oñate took over a pueblo called Ohke. Ohke's Indian inhabitants had to move out and create new shelters as best they could.

After drawing an outline of the new church on the ground, the workers put up a few adobe bricks and a temporary altar. The Spaniards then held as lavish a dedication ceremony as circumstances allowed. Afterward, an unstated number of Pueblo leaders assembled in what had been Ohke's principal kiva. There they listened to the interpreters go through the Spanish messages. That done, the Indians showed their submission by another kissing of hands.

Again, there is no record of what the Pueblos thought, but surely they talked things over in their own way. Some of them argued that they had given in too easily.

Among those who spoke up in favor of resistance were the people of Acoma. Their spectacular pueblo was located sixty miles southwest of present-day Albuquerque on the flat top of a butte whose walls of red rock were 350 feet high. Only a couple of risky foot trails led to the village.

In December 1598, three months after the meeting at Ohke, about twenty Spanish soldiers stopped at the Acoma fields near the base of the butte. Leaving their horses under guard, they followed a Pueblo guide up one of the breathtaking trails to the town. There they demanded food.

As the provisions were being collected, the soldiers scattered out, peering curiously into the stone dwellings. A sudden war cry brought Indian fighters swarming into the streets. In an instant, thirteen Spaniards lay dead. In desperation a few others jumped off the edge of the butte. Those who landed on

Acoma Pueblo, located on top of a high, red, cliff-sided mesa, was the scene of a fierce battle between the Spanish and the Indians. *Seaver Center, Natural History Museum of Los Angeles County.*

the rocks more than three hundred feet below died instantly. But a couple fell onto a big dune of deep, soft sand. Though badly shaken, they reached their horses and rode as fast as they could to Ohke (by then renamed San Gabriel) and reported what had happened.

In January 1599, a vengeful troop of seventy Spaniards forced their way up the risky trails to the high-perched town. A wild, two-day battle ended with the destruction of the village. There is no record of how many Indians were killed. Five hundred or so Pueblo men, women, and children were herded as captives to Santo Domingo, where the Franciscans had established their headquarters.

As punishment, twenty-four Pueblo men of fighting age each had his right foot chopped off. Small children were taken to orphanages in Mexico. Boys, women, and older men became household slaves or field-workers.

The destruction of Acoma and the severe punishments were supposed to frighten Pueblos everywhere into obedience. But more violence was needed to suppress them. An uprising by the southern Pueblos east of Socorro had to be beaten down in a battle that took the lives of nine hundred Indians—or so the reports say. After that the Pueblos became obedient.

For Juan de Oñate, New Mexico was a disaster. He and his soldiers explored extensively but found no mines. The expense of bringing in supplies by cart and pack train across more than six hundred miles of desert shrank his fortune at an alarming rate. His colonists complained bitterly. They said they had been tricked into coming. Irrigation supplies and cropland were not nearly as good as they had been told. Perhaps even more depressing was their isolation from the rest of the world.

Only the strenuous objections of the Franciscans kept New Mexico from being abandoned. The priests claimed to have baptized thousands of Indian children. Thousands more awaited salvation. Surely that great duty should not be given up. The king agreed, and New Mexico was changed into an ecclesiastic or church colony supported by the royal family. Oñate was replaced by a new governor. In 1610, the capital was moved from San Gabriel to a more central location and named Santa Fe. The Franciscans immediately set about expanding their influence, but demands on the Franciscan order from all parts of the world were heavy. It is doubtful that there were ever more than thirty-five or so priests in the province, which reached as far west as the Hopi villages, at any one time.

Franciscan friars tried hard to convert the Pueblos to Catholicism. The Indians resisted stubbornly. *From* Kiva, Cross, and Crown. *Courtesy, Dr. John L. Kessell.*

The friars did bring some improvements with them. They passed out metal buckets, sharp axes, and knives that enabled a hunter to skin a rabbit in record time. They brought donkeys, which could carry firewood down from the mountains. New foods were also introduced: wheat, melons, chili peppers, and peaches and apples.

At the missions, the friars taught children how to read and write. The children learned how to sing and play musical instruments at church services. Boys and young men became blacksmiths and carpenters. Guided by the friars, the Indians built churches even more awesome than some of the great houses at Chaco Canyon.

The gains came at a price. Spanish law allowed both the church and the civil government in the Americas to demand tribute (a type of tax) from the native people they oversaw. The Indians paid the tribute in the form of labor, food, and merchandise, such as piñon nuts and antelope hides that could be sent to Mexico for trading. To meet the burdens, the Pueblos often had to neglect their own houses and fields.

Far more alarming to the Indians was the determination of the friars to crush the Pueblo religion. For a thousand or more years, the natives of the Southwest had been a desert people. Rain was the overwhelming necessity of their lives. Their intricate dances, chants, and other rituals were their way of asking the great powers of the weather to send them what all living things need most—water. They believed that their prayers, carried to the One Above by the kachina spirits, helped the entire thirsty world and not just themselves.

The Pueblos tried to hide the sacred ceremonies from the priests by performing them late at night in the underground kivas. The Spaniards sensed what was going on, but they were

Kachina rituals include exotic, colorful dances and chants. Their purpose is to bring rain and harmony to the world. This dance was photographed at the Hopi town of Walpi.
Photographer, Kate Cory. Smoki Museum, courtesy, Fran Hunnold.

so busy quarreling among themselves over power that for many years they let the Indians' disobedience slide without severe punishment.

During the late 1660s, the Spanish mood swung back toward ruthlessness. Soldiers accompanied by friars raided the kivas for sacred masks, colorful costumes, and gaily feathered prayer sticks. They tossed these sacred objects onto piles in the plazas and burned them while the Indians watched helplessly.

These drawings show a few Kachina masks. The friars called them heathenish and destroyed huge piles of them. *From Kiva, Cross, and Crown.* *Courtesy, Dr. John L. Kessell.*

The climax came in 1675. Forty-seven Indians from different pueblos were arrested and charged with using witchcraft to kill a dozen or so Spaniards, one of them an aged priest. In those days many people in many countries believed in witches. In 1692, in Salem, Massachusetts, for example, twenty people and two dogs were executed for being witches. Three of the accused Pueblo Indians in New Mexico were hanged in public, another killed himself, and the rest were whipped until blood streamed down their backs.

The Indian reaction was extraordinary. Normally, Pueblo towns declined to cooperate with each other. After the cruelties of 1675, however, the outraged victims began plotting ways for all the Indian towns to work together to get rid of their oppressors.

A carefully planned revolt erupted in August 1680. Numerically, the odds favored the Indians. There may have been as many as 15,000 of them, whereas there were no more than 2,500 Spanish subjects living in Santa Fe and in scattered ranches and villages throughout the Rio Grande Valley. However, the Indians lacked guns and horses. The Spaniards had refused to let them have those things for fear it would make them dangerous. But they were dangerous without them. Skillfully directed squads of Indians swept across New Mexico's ranches, through towns, and into Santa Fe.

The Spaniards, caught in the capital city, made a fort of the Palace of the Governors. It was a long, low building with a large horse corral behind it. The Spaniards and loyal Indians who gathered there resisted bravely for two days. The rebels diverted the creek that supplied the palace with water. Meanwhile, Indian reinforcements kept arriving from Taos and other distant pueblos. In despair, the Spanish forces burst out of the palace and rushed for freedom. The daring move caught the Indians unprepared. Besides, they had already suffered heavy casualties and were unwilling to risk more. They were satisfied with the Spaniards' just getting out of New Mexico—which they did, accompanied by many frightened Indians from the southern pueblos.

All told, twenty-one out of thirty-three missionary priests and 375 colonists and soldiers were killed. Many ranches lay open to plundering. Apaches and Navajos responded gleefully, running off herds of sheep, cattle, and horses. Other Spanish horses escaped from the deserted town and farms and turned wild. Horses soon spread throughout the American West.

The Pueblos could not sustain their victory. Once the Spaniards were gone, the alliance fell apart. Some of the Indian
leaders took to acting like Spanish tyrants, riding around in
fancy carriages and demanding tribute. Most went back to
their villages. There they began to have second thoughts.
Where were they going to get new supplies of tools and other
conveniences they had grown used to? Without help from the
Spanish soldiers, how were they going to fight off the increasingly bold Apaches and Navajos?

Twelve years passed before a newly appointed governor,
Don Diego de Vargas, launched a vigorous effort to reconquer
New Mexico. Several Pueblo Indians went with him as allies.
Don Diego de Vargas and his men negotiated peace when they
could and fought when they had to. By the end of 1692, it
seemed that victory had been achieved. But when the new civil
government and the Franciscans reimposed rules against the
native religion, there were fierce Indian uprisings in 1694 and
again in 1696. The uprisings were put down, but at a heavy
cost.

The most bitter reaction came from the Hopis in 1700. Christian Indians from Awatavi, the easternmost of the Hopi villages, had rebuilt the town's partially destroyed Catholic
church and invited new Franciscan missionaries to live with
them. Before the priests arrived, a hundred resentful warriors,
most of them from the Hopis' principal pueblo of Oraibi,
launched a surprise night attack on the church, where the
Christian Indians were meeting. They killed the men and distributed the women and children among the other Hopi towns.
After that, no missionaries reached the Hopis for another 150
years.

In 1680, the Pueblos revolted against religious oppression and labor forced on them by the Spaniards. Not until 1696 did Don Diego de Vargas succeed in putting an end to the last flares of resistance. *Artist unknown. Museum of New Mexico, negative 11409.*

The Hopi pueblo of Walpi perches spectacularly on the southern tip of First Mesa in Arizona. *George Alexander Grant, National Park Service.*

Twenty years of violence and uncertainty (1680–1700) had completely disrupted the Pueblo communities. Many towns had been deserted. Some of the refugees had gone to live with the Hopis. Several had actually joined the Navajos. The various Zuni villages, joined by frightened people from the Rio Grande area, formed a single big new town on top of Dowa Yalanne (Corn Mountain). Other new towns took form where none had been before. Laguna, New Mexico, is one that still exists.

Always, the Pueblos had prayed for harmony in the world. Now disorder seemed to rule. Could harmony and safety ever return?

This spur is a powerful symbol. It stands for the good things the Spanish brought to the Indians—livestock, many new crafts and foods, and a knowledge of reading and writing. It can also stand for the trampling out of freedom. *Photographer, George H. H. Huey.*

10

The Long Road to Recovery

The revolts persuaded the Spaniards that gentleness might be more productive than force in dealing with the Pueblo Indians. Accordingly, de Vargas canceled most of the tributes the Indians had to pay to the church and government officers. The king "generously" granted four square leagues of ground to each village—land that the Indians had freely wandered across for many hundreds of years. Finally, the priests pretended not to notice the Pueblos' underground rituals.

Pleased by the turn of events, the Indians grew more cooperative. Famous early-day Christian martyrs were accepted as patron saints of many of the villages. The saints' traditional birthdays were celebrated with feasts and games. Many Pueblos accepted baptism and entered the Catholic Church. Yet most of the "converts" also retained their ties to their Pueblo faith. In their opinion, there was nothing wrong in benefiting from what they considered the best parts of both religions.

After peace had come, Spanish colonists began settling on little farms near the Pueblos. Gradually the two groups took to sharing certain chores, such as cleaning irrigation ditches. Once a year they traveled together, in small parties, to attend the huge trade fair the colonial government established at Taos in 1723.

The fair was exciting. Plains Indians rode west from as far as Kansas to attend. Pueblos from throughout New Mexico were on hand. Spanish merchants arrived with laden pack trains. There was lots of merrymaking. Even today, Pueblos perform dances they learned from the Plains Indians at the fairs. They call the dances Comanche dances, although they may have been borrowed from any of the Plains tribes.

Soon mixed parties of Hispanics and Pueblos were traveling

The Comanches were the feared raiders of the Great Plains. But after being defeated in a fierce battle with Pueblo and Spanish troops, they became trading partners with some of the Pueblos. *Artist, Roy Anderson. Courtesy, Pecos National Historical Park.*

The Pueblos borrowed dances from several of the Plains tribes, but they called them all Comanche dances. They are still performed in some plazas. *Museum of New Mexico, negative 3564.*

together onto the Plains. Their intent was to hunt buffalo and trade with any agreeable Indians they met. After the early 1700s, those were probably Comanches. Many scattered bands of that hard-riding, fierce-fighting tribe were migrating out of Wyoming. They were pushing the Apaches southward toward Old Mexico and westward into southern Arizona.

Sometimes the Comanches were willing to trade with the Pueblos and Hispanics. But there was no real peace. Comanche war parties would suddenly strike hard at a pueblo. They'd loot the town of food and horses, but mostly they stole Pueblo children. They sold the little ones to tribes that raised them to be slaves.

Working under their own war captains, members of the looted pueblo would join a few ragged Hispanic soldiers and set off in pursuit. They seldom caught the guilty raiders. But now and then they would stumble onto a different group.

Frustrated, they would charge at it and, if victorious, steal some of its children. They'd sell them as slaves in New Mexico.

Such random violence spread anger far and wide. Hatreds in New Mexico grew so intense that the officials in Mexico City launched campaigns against all the horse-riding Indians of the High Plains. Juan Bautista de Anza, the skilled frontiersman who had recently founded the city of San Francisco in California, marched against the major band of the Comanches. He defeated them, killed their great chief, Cuerno Verde (Green Horn), and made the survivors sign a stiff peace treaty.

Farther south other Mexican generals pounded the Apaches into submission. For the next forty years, New Mexico was more peaceful than it had been since the days of the Pueblo revolt.

In spite of the peace, the late 1700s and early 1800s were sorrowful years for the Pueblos. Crop-killing droughts devastated New Mexico. Diseases brought from Europe by the Spaniards added to the tragedy. The Pueblos had built up no immunity against such terrors as smallpox, tuberculosis, or measles. Epidemics spread rapidly through the crowded, unsanitary pueblos. The Pueblo population dropped from the 60,000 Coronado had encountered to about 9,000. The number of towns shrank from almost a hundred to twenty-three.

Meanwhile Spanish power in the New World was also shrinking. In 1821 Mexico became independent. The young nation made a lot of promises. It declared that the Pueblo Indians were full citizens of the republic. It confirmed the Pueblos' land grants. But it couldn't control the ranchers who began moving huge herds of sheep into New Mexico. Inevitably the animals trespassed on the Pueblo land grants and trampled many sacred sites into dust. And Mexico was unable to control the unconquered Indians who had sensed the confusion and had launched new raids. The once great Pueblo of Pecos was abandoned by its inhabitants, as were a couple of other towns. Before long only nineteen pueblos remained in New Mexico, plus the remote Hopi villages in Arizona.

Hope for relief came from the United States, which went to war with Mexico in 1846. Within months General Stephen Watts Kearny had led a small column of Americans into Santa Fe. Grandly he promised to protect the Southwest, which was now American territory, from all Indian dangers. But he didn't realize how tough the "horse Indians" could be. Full peace did not come to Pueblo country until the 1870s.

In the relative safety, the pueblo towns spread out. The inhabitants tore down the upper stories, which were costly to maintain. Doorways were opened onto the streets. Gardens containing corn, beans, and chili peppers appeared between the houses or in plots at the edge of towns.

Jemez Pueblo after 1870. With no enemies to fear, doors opened onto the streets. Ladders still led to the roofs, scenes of much work and lolling around. Note the drying chili peppers in the foreground and the Spanish-style ovens on the far side of the street.
Photographer, Ben Wittick. Museum of New Mexico, negative 16097.

In 1880–81, the California-bound Santa Fe Railroad was built across New Mexico and Arizona. At first the Pueblos felt that another disaster had struck them.

Many Indians earned wages as construction workers, but most of those jobs evaporated when the railroad reached California. Regular train service also delivered a serious blow to Indian crafts. Blankets woven in the kivas by hand could not compete with machine-made products. Women who carried their pottery to wayside depots, hoping to sell a piece or two to the train passengers, often could get no more than a quarter for their offerings. Many quit making pottery.

The railroad also brought in crowds of white land speculators. They knew land prices were going up. Some built cabins on Pueblo lands just as if the area were a part of the American public domain and open to homesteading. Then they sold the cabins to unwary customers. The Pueblos tried to fight back with lawsuits, but their grants had never been officially surveyed and they generally lost.

Meanwhile the United States government established schools to help Americanize the Indians. As soon as the children were old enough, they were required to leave their homes and go to distant boarding schools. Sometimes soldiers would help drag them away if the parents resisted or tried to hide the children. At the schools the boys had their long hair cut short. Both boys and girls had to wear uniforms of cheap American clothes. They were fed strange foods. They were forced to speak English at all times.

The girls were taught to cook and sew American style. The boys learned crafts such as blacksmithing, metal fabricating, and carpentry. Those were gains. But they were not allowed time off to return home and learn the secret dances and rituals of their native religion, even though America was supposed to be a land of religious freedom. Being prevented from participating in the ancient customs was a definite loss.

To fight back, the Pueblo villages gave up some of their autonomy and formed the All Indian Pueblo Council. Its roots went back to the council that had launched the great anti-Spanish revolt of 1680. This time they fought their battles in the courts and began winning some cases. Many complicated land and water problems remained. However, in 1970 the government actually gave back land instead of taking it. This helped replace acreage that had been severely damaged by overgrazing and overlogging by white and Hispanic ranchers.

The Indians won a voice in running their children's schools by gaining control of the local school boards. Most of the schools ran only through the eighth grade. To go to high school, most young Indians had to travel long distances. Some of them managed to continue on to college. A few went on to graduate schools.

The seeds of the most spectacular changes were planted by two white archaeologists. One was named Jesse Walter Fewkes. The other was Edgar Hewett. In the late 1800s, workers employed by Fewkes were digging into the ancient ruins of Sityatki at the base of what the Hopi Indians call First Mesa. Hewett's workers were simultaneously excavating Tyuonyi, located in a deep canyon in the rugged mountains behind the Rio Grande Pueblo of San Ildefonso. The two sites were nearly two hundred miles apart, but both men were struck by the same marvelous idea at approximately the same time.

One of Walter Fewkes's diggers was a man named Lesou. He came from the Hopi town of Walpi. His wife was named Nampeyo. She was a native of the town of Hano, which adjoins

Walpi. Hano is not a Hopi town but was founded by fugitives fleeing from the Rio Grande Valley after de Vargas had conquered the rebels of 1680. Even today, three hundred years later, the people of Hano keep pretty much to themselves and still speak their own language, called Tewa. But young people from Walpi and Hano do marry sometimes.

Fewkes asked Lesou if his wife, who occasionally made ceramics, could duplicate some of the ancient pots his men were digging up at Sityatki. Nampeyo agreed to try. She found the kind of clay and temper that suited her. She mixed the elements with water, smoothed out the results, and let it dry to the proper stiffness. Rolling and then winding coil after coil, she copied the shapes of the Sityatki pots that were brought to her. Lesou painted on the designs with a brush made of fine, thin yucca fibers. Together they fired the pots in a kiln they built behind their house—a new kiln for every firing.

In time husband and wife, influenced by Sityatki models, began creating pots of their own. What emerged were exquisite red-gold-orange-black vessels that are a stunning combination of new and old.

At first the pair marketed their wares at a nearby trading post. Tourists visiting the Hopi mesas discovered them, and soon the demand was greater than they could fill. Other Indian potters added their interpretations. The entire area had a new source of income.

As Nampeyo aged, she went blind. She also lost some of her powers of speech. But she could still mold pots according to the visions that came to her. Nampeyo and Lesou's children followed their lead, and the Sityatki tradition remains strong.

Meanwhile, at San Ildefonso, Edgar Hewett was talking to one of his workers, Julian Martinez, about the unusual black pots his workers were finding at the ancient pueblo of Tyuonyi. Could Julian and his wife, Maria, find out how those pots had been made? Maria, who was already an expert potter, agreed to try.

Through endless experiments, they found that if they made a pot of a particular kind of clay and fired it very slowly in a smoldering blanket of sheep manure, it would come out black. After more experiments, they discovered that if Julian applied a rough black paint to sections of Maria's highly polished, gorgeously shaped pots, the painted portion would come from the kiln coarse and dull. Unexpectedly, this matte, or rough finish, and the gleaming, polished sections worked with each other to form an eye-catching contrast. Julian heightened the contrast by carving designs into the matte with his knife. The wonderful shape and form of Maria's pots heightened the appeal of the designs while the designs emphasized the exquisite shapes of the vessels.

Potters Maria and Julian Martinez of San Ildefonso invented new designs and styles in pottery. Their work is cherished by collectors throughout the world. *Museum of New Mexico, negative 30466.*

After Julian died, their daughter-in-law Santana and Maria's son Popovi Da became her assistants, adding touches of their own. But Maria was the leader of the family project. She was taken to world fairs to demonstrate her black-on-black techniques. Today, for many people, Maria Martinez is the leading name in Pueblo pottery.

Fine pottery, much of it drawing inspiration from ancient examples, is now an important source of income for today's Pueblo Indians. *Photographer, Stephen Trimble.*

Their dazzling innovations in jewelry, painting, and making colorful kachina dolls have given the Pueblos a worldwide reputation for artistry. But not every Pueblo Indian can be or wants to be an artist. Large numbers of them seek jobs that pay regular wages, from physical labor to clerking in government offices. Some start small businesses. Pueblos that have recreational lands welcome, for a small fee, non-Indian picnickers, hikers, and fishermen. Casinos for tourists have been the most profitable pursuit. The casinos are entirely managed by the Pueblos on whose land they stand.

Those who find jobs away from their home pueblos face special problems. They have trouble getting enough time off from their work to rush home for the village's complicated ceremonial dances. They miss rehearsals. Their costumes lack some of the finishing touches. Elders fear that too many shortcuts will cause these hurry-up people to lose some of their basic "Indianness."

Feast day at the pueblo of Santa Clara. During the summer, when the kachina spirits are home among the clouds or on the mountaintops, the townspeople perform unmasked dances in the plazas. Most of the entertainments are open to non-Indian spectators.
Photographer, Stephen Trimble.

All dressed up for a feast day celebration at the pueblo of San Juan. *Photographer, Stephen Trimble.*

Since government schools used to require that the children speak only English, many children came to feel that their native languages were somehow inferior. When they grew up, they discovered that most business outside the pueblos was conducted in English. Television encouraged still more English. What's the use, some ask, of learning their own tongues?

Elders retort that language is a necessary part of their culture and of their personal sense of identity. Maxine Toya of Jemez Pueblo is one of several traditionalists who puts this conviction into action. She is a potter and also teaches in the Jemez elementary school. Like several other pueblos, the people of Jemez have gained control of their local school board, so Maxine is free to experiment. She opens and closes each school day with lessons in the culture and in speaking Towa, the native language of the Jemez people.

Maxine Toya also takes her fifth-graders on field trips to show them where she and her mother, Marie Romero, find the special clay they use in making their famous pottery and statuettes of Pueblo storytellers. Clay connects them to the strengths of the earth, mother and daughter believe. They are convinced, too, that "Indianness," which includes their native language, helped their people survive the past and will carry them safely into the future.

Luckily they may be right. After many years of shrinking, Pueblo populations are growing again.

Maxine Toya (above), who teaches fifth-grade classes at Jemez, wants her students to remember their Indian heritage while learning American subjects. She opens and closes each school day by teaching Towa, their native language. And Maxine's mother, Marie Romero, (below) an accomplished potter, teaches traditional crafts during field days. *Both photographs, Nancy Dahl.*

Old and new. A Santa Clara grandfather and his grandchildren. *Seaver Center, Natural History Museum of Los Angeles County.*

Glossary

Anasazi The ancestors of today's Pueblo Indians. In Navajo, the word means "Ancient Ones" or sometimes "Ancient Enemies."

archaeology The science that studies the material remains of past peoples in order to understand their lives and cultures.

arroyo A gash cut into dry hillsides or the bottom of small valleys by runoff from sudden, heavy storms.

atlatl A throwing stick used by prehistoric hunters to increase the range and impact of their spears.

effigy A small, often crude image, generally made of stone or cloth, representing someone hated by the maker.

firing A process for hardening pottery by subjecting it to intense heat in a kiln.

great house Informally, the many-storied, multiroomed apartment houses—the "room blocks"—left by the Anasazi.

Hano A town located among the Hopi of First Mesa, Arizona. It was founded by fugitives from the Rio Grande Valley during the Pueblo revolt of 1680–96.

Hispanic An early Spanish settler of the Southwest, especially New Mexico.

Hopi A Pueblo tribe whose Anasazi ancestors settled on and near the long fingers of land extending south from Black Mesa, Arizona. The Hopis are widely known for their artistic achievements and their skill at farming arid land.

kachina One of the supernatural beings who visit the kivas during the winter to participate in the ceremonies that teach the Pueblos harmonious behavior and help persuade the gods to send rain. Because the kachinas are invisible, they are represented by chosen men wearing colorful masks and costumes.

kiva An underground or partially underground ceremonial structure. Generally circular but sometimes rectangular, kivas are still used by Pueblos, mostly male, for social and religious gatherings.

maize The Indian name for corn. It was first cultivated in central Mexico thousands of years ago and carried slowly north.

mano A shaped stone tool held in a miller's hand and used to crush seeds or corn into coarse flour for cooking.

metate A slab of flat stone with a basin or trough in its center. Seeds or corn were placed in the basin and crushed with the mano.

obsidian A volcanic glass, generally shiny black. It fractures easily into large, sharp-edged flakes used by many Indian groups for making knife blades and projectile points.

pit house A dwelling, usually in colder climates, sunken from one to three feet into the ground. It was covered by a superstructure of pickets daubed with mud and rocks. Early models were conical and entered through a tunnel. Later, roofs were flat. Smoke left and people entered the house through holes in the roof.

rubble mound A pile of shaped stone where masonry walls have collapsed and then been covered by windblown sand or mud from occasional floods.

sipapu A mythical hole through which people climbed from the third world onto the earth. The Hopi *sipapu* was located in the gorge of the Little Colorado. Many Anasazi houses contained small holes in their floors, symbolic of the *sipapu*.

talus house A talus consists of a mass of chunks of rock that have fallen from a cliff. The Anasazi occasionally built small villages on top of or adjacent to these mounds, perhaps because the talus rocks were of a convenient size for construction work.

temper Fine sand, ground rock, or finely ground pieces of pottery that is added to wet clay as it is being prepared for making a pot. The temper, as it is called, helps keep the clay from cracking as it cools after being fired.

travertine A form of limestone carried in solution with water. When deposited on other rocks, branches, or anything else, it forms a hard, often picturesque shield over the object.

travois A platform between two long poles whose forward ends are attached to either side of a horse or big dog. The back ends drag on the ground. Loads of meat, buffalo hides, or whatever the Indians wanted to move were lashed onto the platform between the poles.

yucca A desert plant with many uses. Its leaves were tough, long, and needle-pointed at their ends. The points served as a kind of awl. The Anasazi wove sandals and mats out of cordage made from the leaf fibers. They roasted and ate the heart of some varieties. They made soap and a laxative out of its roots.

Zuni An Anasazi/Pueblo group that occupied the southwest section of Anasazi territory. They were the first North American Indians Coronado met during his 1540 search for gold and jewels. Their background is puzzling, for their language is unlike that used by any other group anywhere, except possibly a small California band.

Bibliography

(The initials SPMA stand for Southwestern Parks and Monuments Association)

Ambler, J. Richard. *The Anasazi: Prehistoric Peoples of the Four Corners Region*. Flagstaff: Museum of Northern Arizona Press, 1989.

———. *Archaeological Assessment, Navajo National Monument*. Santa Fe: Southwest Cultural Resources Center, National Park Service, 1985.

Barry, Patricia. *Bandalier National Monument*. Tucson: SPMA, 1990.

Bezy, John, and Joseph P. Sanchez (eds.). *Pecos, Gateway to Pueblo and Plains*. Tucson: SPMA, 1988.

Breternitz, David A., and Jack Smith. *Mesa Verde, The Green Table*. Casper, Wyo.: World-Wide Research and Publishing Co., 1972.

Ceram, C. W. *The First American: A Story of North American Archaeology*. New York: NAL/Dutton, 1992.

Dittert, Alfred Jr., and Fred Plog. *Generations in Clay: Pueblo Pottery of the American Southwest*. Flagstaff: Northland Publishing, 1980.

Dockstader, Frederick J. *The Kachina and the White Man: The Influence of White Culture on the Hopi Kachina Cult*. Albuquerque: University of New Mexico Press, 1985.

Handbook of North American Indians. Vol. 9. Washington, D.C.: Smithsonian Institution, 1979.

Kessell, John L. *Kiva, Cross and Crown: The Pecos Indians and New Mexico*. Washington, D.C.: National Park Service, 1979. Reprint, SPMA, 1995.

Lister, Robert H., and Florence C. Lister. *Those Who Came Before: Southwestern Archaeology in the National Park System*. Tucson: SPMA (rev. ed.), 1994.

———. *Earl Morris and Southwestern Archaeology.* Tucson: SPMA, 1993.

———. *Chaco Canyon Archaeology and Archaeologists.* Albuquerque: University of New Mexico Press, 1981.

McNitt, Frank. *Richard Wetherill, Anasazi.* Albuquerque: University of New Mexico Press, 1966.

Murphy, Daniel O. *Salinas Pueblo Missions National Monument.* Tucson: SPMA, 1992.

———. *El Morro National Monument.* Tucson: SPMA, 1989.

Noble, David G. *Zuni and El Morro, Past and Present.* Santa Fe: Ancient City Press, 1993.

———. (ed.). *New Light on Chaco Canyon.* Santa Fe: Annual Bulletin of the School of American Research, 1984.

Noble, David G., and Tse Ya Kin. *Understanding the Anasazi of Mesa Verde and Hovenweep.* Santa Fe: Ancient City Press, 1992.

Powell, Shirley, and George G. Gumerman. *People of the Mesa: The Archaeology of Black Mesa, Arizona.* Carbondale, Ill.: SPMA and Southern Illinois University Press, 1987.

Riley, Carrol D. *Rio del Norte: People of the Upper Rio Grande from the Earliest Times to the Pueblo Revolt.* Salt Lake City: University of Utah Press, 1995.

Rippeteau, Bruce Estes. *A Colorado Book of the Dead, the Prehistoric Era.* Denver: The Colorado Historical Society, 1979.

Roberts, David. "The Old Ones of the Southwest." National Geographic Society, April 1996.

Sando, Joe S. *Pueblo Nations: Eight Centuries of Pueblo Indian History.* Santa Fe: Clear Light Publishers, 1992.

Simmons, Leo W. (ed.). *Sun Chief: The Autobiography of a Hopi Indian.* New Haven: Yale University Press, 1963.

Spicer, Edward H. *Cycles of Conquest: The Impact of Spain, Mexico, and the United States on Indians of the Southwest, 1533–1960.* Tucson: The University of Arizona Press, 1962.

Strutin, Michelle. *Chaco: A Cultural Legacy.* Tucson: SPMA, 1994.

Thompson, Ian. *The Towers of Hovenweep.* Mesa Verde National Park: Mesa Verde Museum Association, 1993.

Thybony, Scott. *Aztec Ruins National Monument.* Tucson: SPMA, 1992.

Trimble, Stephen. *The People, Indians of the American Southwest.* Santa Fe: School of American Research Press, 1993.

———. *Talking with the Clay: The Art of Pueblo Pottery.* Santa Fe: School of American Research Press, 1987.

Trimble, Stephen, Harvey Lloyd, and the Indian People of the Southwest. *Our Voices, Our Land.* Flagstaff: Northland Publishing, 1993.

Webb, William, and Robert A. Weinstein. *Dwellers at the Source. South-Western Indian Photography of A. C. Vroman, 1895–1904.* Albuquerque: University of New Mexico Press, 1992.

Wright, Barton. *The Unchanging Hopi: An Artist's Interpretation.* Flagstaff: Northland Publishing, 1975.

Wright, Barton, Marnie Gaede, and Marc Gaede. *The Hopi Photographs of Kate Cory, 1905–1912.* Albuquerque: University of New Mexico Press, 1988.

Index

Page numbers in italics refer to photos